Battles
of the Bible

Battles
of the Bible

CHARTWELL
BOOKS, INC.

A QUANTUM BOOK

Published in 2009 by Chartwell Books
A division of Book Sales Inc.
114 Northfield Avenue
Edison, New Jersey 08837, USA

ISBN-13: 978-0-7858-2527-2
ISBN-10: 0785825274

This book is produced by
Quantum Books
6 Blundell Street
London N7 9BH

QUMBOTB

Printed in China by Midas Printing Limited

Publisher: Anastasia Cavouras
Editor: Sarah Burnside
Fulfilment Assistant: Samantha Warrington
Designer: Richard Shiner
Production: Rohana Yusof

Contents

Introduction

The Ancient Israelites, fleeing from their cruel oppressors, faced countless enemies, harsh conditions, and hostile terrain as they struggled to carve out an empire in the Promised Land and embrace their destiny as God's chosen children.

Led sometimes by the unlikeliest of warriors, the armies of the Old Testament became embroiled in battles, wars, and conflicts that had an overwhelming influence on the course of ancient history.

The biblical world was one of bloodshed and conflict, from the time of the Exodus, when Moses outmaneuvered Pharaoh's formidable army to take the Israelites away from their long-suffered slavery to the land that the Lord himself had promised them, to the terrible sacking of Masada by the Romans, ending the Jewish revolt against Hellenistic rule with great bloodshed.

Under the command of Joshua and the Judges, the Israelites invaded Canaan, their mounting victories including the fall of Jericho, the battle of Ai and the defeat of Sisera. After many years in the wilderness, the Israelites finally settled in their Promised Land.

In the time of Saul, the first king of the newly established Israel, a new threat loomed from the Philistines, culminating in the Battle of Michmash and his ultimate defeat at Gilboa.

The reigns of David and Solomon brought their own dangers, including David's capture of Jerusalem and the split of the Israelites' kingdom into Judah and Israel, culminating in the eventual fall of Israel and the siege of Samaria.

The Israelites' enemies were powerful and mighty, with the Egyptians, Assyrians, Babylonians, and Romans among their number. Alexander the Great swept through biblical territories, with few able to stand up to his army's might, while the Persians defeated the Babylonians and Jerusalem was sacked by the Romans, killing a reported 1.1 million people.

After the Babylonian empire was dissolved and the Jews were allowed to return to Jerusalem, new battles erupted as first the Romans besieged them, and then the pagan Greek culture offended their religious sensibilities.

The Bible's many tales of military action provide the backdrop against which its most famous incidents took place: the fight between David and Goliath, the story of Samson and Delilah, Judith and Holofernes, and the journeys of Paul among so many others. The conditions and terrain, along with the military techniques and weapons available to the warriors of each of its various kingdoms, contributed to the epic clashes that shaped both the power and geography of the ancient world.

The Ancient Near East
in the Third Millennium

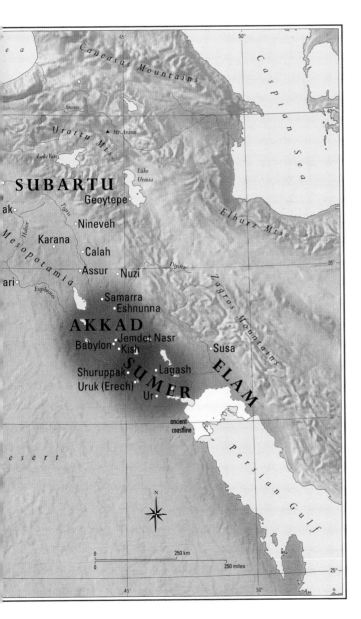

Left: As the timeline
of the Bible began,
powerful civilisations
had established
their dominance
throughout the
'Fertile Crescent'.

The Promised Land   9

The Promised Land

When the Children of Israel, the future Israelites, were led out of Egypt by Moses and his brother, Aaron, they were escaping from what the Bible presents as cruel, exploitative masters who had kept them in misery and slavery for some 16 generations. But freedom from their insupportable conditions was not the be-all and end-all of it. As the biblical Book of Exodus reveals, the Israelites had a destination and a destiny, although it would be 40 years before they would reach one and fulfill the other.

In the Book of Exodus, Moses and, through him, the Children of Israel were apprised of the Promised Land of Canaan even before they left the slavery of their Egyptian masters. In Chapter 3, Verse 8, God speaks to Moses from the burning bush, saying: "And I am come down to deliver them out of the hand of the Egyptians, and to bring them up out of that land unto a good land and a large, unto a land flowing with milk and honey...."

This was a highly tempting image of their future home but, as the Israelites soon

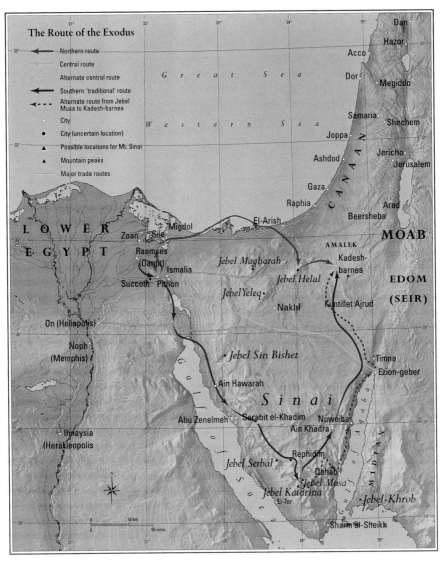

The Route of the Exodus

Northern route
Central route
Alternate central route
Southern 'traditional' route
Alternate route from Jebel Musa to Kadesh-barnea
City
City (uncertain location)
Possible locations for Mt. Sinai
Mountain peaks
Major trade routes

Dan
Hazor
Acco
Great Sea
Dor
Megiddo
Western Sea
Samaria
Shechem
Joppa
Jericho
Ashdod
Jerusalem
Gaza
Raphia
Arad
Beersheba
El-Arish
MOAB
Migdol
Zoan
Sile
AMALEK
Kadesh-barnea
Raamses
(Qantir)
Ismalia
Jebel Magharah
EDOM
(SEIR)
Succoth
Pithon
Jebel Helal
Jebel Yeleq
Kuntillet Ajrud
Nakhl
On (Heliopolis)
Noph
(Memphis)
Jebel Sin Bishet
Timna
Ezion-geber
Ain Hawarah
Sinai
Ihnaysia
(Herakleopolis
Abu Zenelmeh
Sorabit el-Khadim
Nuweiba
Ain Khadra
Gulf of Suez
Rephidim
Jebel Serbal
Dahab
Jebel Musa
MIDIAN
Jebel Katarina
El-Tor
Jebel-Khrob
Gulf of Aqaba
Sharm el-Sheikh

Above: The Israelite religion and identity were founded on their experiences during the Exodus.

discovered, the way to the Promised Land across the Sinai desert, crossing the marshy region to the east of the Nile Delta and then toward the sacred mountain, was long and hard.

In the first place, they were not immune from attack, not only from the Egyptians who pursued them in an effort to recapture their slaves but also from the desert nomads who would prove to be perennial enemies in the future: the Amalekites.

The Amalekites attacked the Israelite camp at Rephidim soon after the Israelites entered what the nomads considered to be their territory: the Sinai Desert. As described in the Book of Exodus, (Chapter 17, Verses 8-13) it was God who orchestrated the Israelites' success in fighting off their attackers:

"Then came Amalek, and fought with Israel in Rephidim. And Moses said unto Joshua, Choose us our men, and go out, fight with Amalek: tomorrow I will stand on the top of the hill with the rod of God in mine hand. So Joshua did as Moses had said to him, and fought with Amalek: and Moses, Aaron, and Hur went up to the top of the hill. And it came to pass, when Moses held up his hand, that Israel prevailed: and when he let down his hand, Amalek prevailed. But Moses' hands were heavy; and they took a stone, and put it under him, and he sat thereon; and Aaron and Hur stayed up his hands, the one on the one side, and the other on the other side; and his hands were steady until the going down of the Sun. And

Opposite: The Book of Exodus is concerned with the journey of the Israelites, led by Moses, from the Egyptian lands across the Sinai Desert.

Joshua discomfited Amalek and his people with the edge of the sword."

But despite this – and other signs of God's care and assistance – the Israelites were not always grateful and sometimes seriously misbehaved, which was why it took 40 years for the Israelites to reach the Promised Land. This was an enormous length of time considering that they were crossing the Sinai desert, a comparatively small expanse of less than 60 square kilometers, 140 times smaller than the Sahara Desert.

This extraordinary time span is explained by the need to allow sufficient years to elapse for the generation of sinners to die off: as the Book of Numbers (Chapter 32, Verse 13) puts it:

"... the Lord's anger was kindled against Israel, and he made them wander in the wilderness 40 years, until all the generation, that had done evil in the sight of the Lord, was consumed."

Arguably the greatest evil done in the sight of the Lord during this time was the building of the Golden Calf during the time Moses was on Mount Sinai receiving the tablets containing the Ten Commandments. Time passed and Moses did not return. After 40 days and 40 nights, the Israelites grew impatient, assumed that Moses had gone missing, and decided to make a god to lead them in his stead.

The gold was melted down from a mass of golden earrings. Once the idol was completed, the Israelites made sacrifices to it and held a celebratory feast that degenerated into an orgy.

Opposite: Moses climbed Mount Sinai to receive the Ten Commandments. While he was gone, the Israelites made a new god to worship.

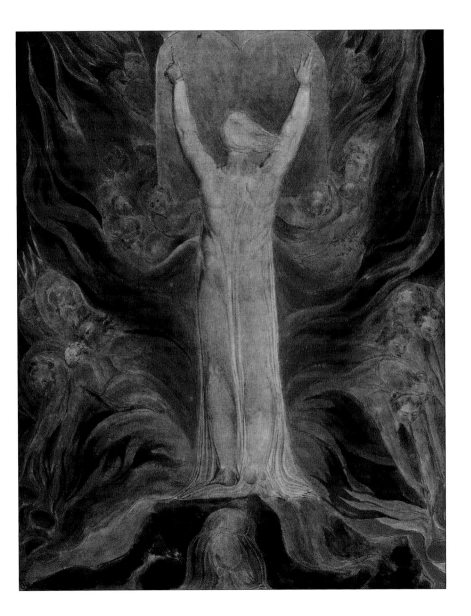

When Moses at length returned, he saw what the Israelites were doing and became so angry that he threw the Golden Calf into a fire, where it melted. Then he ground the gold into a powder, mixed it with water and ordered the people to drink it. Moses also ordered the priests to see that 3,000 of the Israelites were killed for this most serious of transgressions.

But Moses himself was also due for punishment, in his case for disobedience to God's command. During the crossing of Sinai, the Israelites' supply of water ran out and God ordered Moses to speak to a rock, asking it to produce water. But instead of speaking to it, Moses became impatient and hit the rock hard with his staff. Water duly poured out, but Moses still had a penalty to pay. He was to be barred from entering the Promised Land. So was his brother, Aaron, who had been instrumental in the making of the Golden Calf. For, as the Book of Deuteronomy (Chapter 1, Verse 35) states:

"Surely there shall not one of these men of this evil generation see that good land, which I sware to give unto your fathers."

The Book of Deuteronomy goes on to name those who would be permitted to enter the Promised Land of Canaan. One of them was Caleb, of the tribe of Judah, who had "wholly followed the Lord" when he was sent into Canaan to scout out the land. Moses had sent 12 spies into Canaan to gather information, each of whom returned with tales of fierce men and fortified cities. Caleb

Opposite: One man from each of the 12 tribes of Israel was sent into Canaan to gather information and find potential routes for invasion.

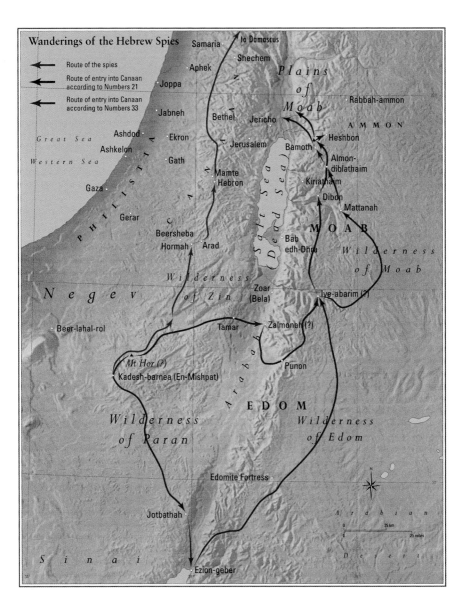

Wanderings of the Hebrew Spies

← Route of the spies

← Route of entry into Canaan according to Numbers 21

← Route of entry into Canaan according to Numbers 33

to Damascus

Samaria
Shechem
Aphek
Joppa
Jabneh
Bethel
Jericho
Jerusalem
Bamoth
Heshbon
Rabbah-ammon
A M M O N
Almon-diblathaim
Kiriathaim
Dibon
Mattanah

Great Sea
Ashdod
Ekron
Ashkelon
Western Sea
Gath
Gaza
Gerar
Mamre
Hebron
Beersheba
Hormah
Arad
Bab edh-Dhra
M O A B
Wilderness of Moab

Salt Sea (Dead Sea)

P H I L I S T I A
C A N A A N

Negev
Wilderness of Zin
Zoar (Bela)
Iye-abarim (?)

Beer-lahal-rol
Tamar
Zalmonah (?)

Mt Hor (?)
Kadesh-barnea (En-Mishpat)
Punon

Arabah
E D O M
Wilderness of Paran
Wilderness of Edom

Edomite Fortress

Arabian

0   25 km
0   25 miles

Jotbathah

S i n a i
D e s e r t

Ezion-geber

Plains of Moab

returned with the news that, as promised, God would be able to deliver the land into the hands of the Israelites. Joshua, of the tribe of Ephraim, another spy who came back with optimistic news, was also among those allowed into the Promised Land. Chapter 1, Verse 38 of Deuteronomy includes a prediction about the role he was destined to play: "He shall cause Israel to inherit it".

So Moses and Aaron died and it was Joshua who led the Israelites into the Promised Land and directed the battles they had to fight in order to make it their own.

The first was the most famous: the battle of Jericho. Before attacking the city, Joshua sent in spies to discover what kind of situation he would have

Opposite: Joshua and Caleb returned bearing the fruits of the land of Canaan and promising an optimistic future for the Israelites there.

to face. Joshua needed to know where the guards were placed, what sort of weapons and armor they carried, whether there were any dissidents in Jericho willing to co-operate with him and where the city's stores of food, water, and other supplies were kept. Most importantly, Joshua sought information about the height and width of Jericho's walls, for these had to be overcome before the Israelite attack could get under way.

Somehow, though, the King of Jericho learned of the presence of Joshua's spies within the city. He ordered them to be found, detained, and brought before him, but a woman called Rahab protected the spies, hiding them in the roof of her house when the king's men came looking for them. The spies got away safely and reported back to Joshua, who decided to proceed with

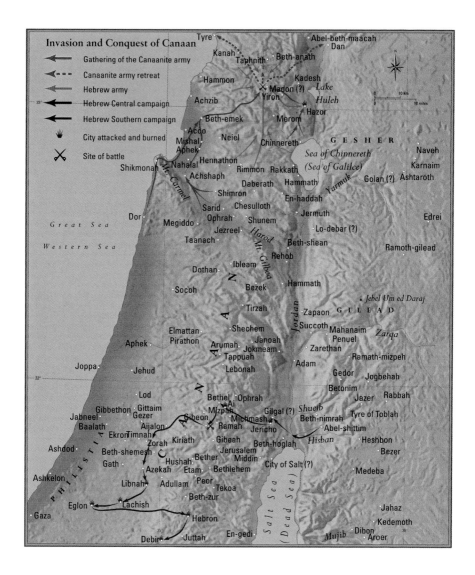

Invasion and Conquest of Canaan

←	Gathering of the Canaanite army
◄---	Canaanite army retreat
←	Hebrew army
←	Hebrew Central campaign
←	Hebrew Southern campaign
♨	City attacked and burned
✕	Site of battle

*Above: The invasion of Canaan began with
Joshua's attack on Jericho from the base at Gilgal.*

the attack.

According to the biblical account of the Siege of Jericho, described in the Book of Joshua, God spoke to Joshua, giving him very specific instructions on how to proceed. The Ark of the Covenant, the holy receptacle that contained the tablets inscribed with the Ten Commandments, was to be carried around the city walls every day for six days, preceded by seven priests carrying rams' horns and followed by the mass of Israelites. On the seventh day, the Sabbath, the whole party was to circle the walls seven times with the priests blowing their horns.

When the horns sounded, the Israelites were instructed to wait for Joshua to give the signal and when he did so, they were to shout as loudly as they could.

At this, the walls of Jericho fell down and, as the Book of Joshua (Chapter 6, Verse 20) recounts: "the people went up into the city, every man straight before him, and they took the city." It appears, though, that everyone inside the city of Jericho – men, women, and children – was killed.

Bible historians have long disagreed about what actually happened at Jericho. It has been suggested that the collapse of its walls – or rather the breaching of the walls by the Israelites – came about through one of two causes, or perhaps through a combination of both. The first postulated reason is that the walls had been cracked and weakened by the earth tremors common in the area, or they had not been kept in proper repair. Another theory has it that the circling of the walls by the priests frightened the people of Jericho at first, but their alarm began to fade after six days of the same behavior when they saw that nothing untoward occurred. The people of Jericho became accustomed to it and relaxed so that when the Israelites attacked in force on the seventh day, they were taken by surprise. Whichever theory holds the key to the victory, Jericho was taken and Joshua was able to proceed to the next battle, at the waters of Merom.

The success scored by Joshua and the Israelites at Jericho was worrying news for the rulers of other cities in Canaan. One of them was Jabin, King of Hazor, who sent warning messages to his fellow monarchs in Madon, Shimron, and Achshaph and to others among the Canaanites, Amorites, Hittites, Perizzites, Jebusites, and Hivites. These kings, it seems, decided on joint action and, according to the Book of Joshua (Chapter 11, Verse 4), "they went out, they and all their hosts with them, much people, even as the sand that is upon the sea shore in multitude with horses and chariots very many."

The various royal armies convened at the waters of Merom (present-day Lake Hula in northern Israel). Among their equipment were the Canaanites' horse-drawn iron chariots, the first the Israelites would encounter. But, again according to Joshua (Chapter 11), God told the Israelites not to be afraid: "for tomorrow about this time will I deliver them up all slain before Israel: thou shalt hough (disable) their horses and burn their chariots with fire." When the battle at Merom was joined,

Opposite: Following instructions given from God himself, the Israelites paraded round the walls of Jericho each day, finally attacking on the seventh.

the Israelites, it seems, attacked with such ferocity that their opponents broke ranks and fled.

The Israelites chased the Canaanites as far as the valley of Mizpeh, where "they smote them, until they left none remaining." To complete his victory, Joshua "did unto them as the Lord bade him" by disabling their horses and burning their chariots.

The capture of Jericho had given Joshua and the Israelites their first solid foothold west of the Jordan river and the first territorial gain in the Promised Land. But despite their crushing defeat of the King of Hazor and his allies, the Canaanites remained a danger to the Israelite forces as long as they controlled the Judean mountains. Although the Israelites had been amazingly successful thus far, they were lightly armed compared to their opponents and lacked the chariots that could be such a deadly force in battle.

Judean mountain country, however, was a much more convenient setting for the kind of warfare the Israelites were fighting. The mountains comprised a natural fortress where the Israelite drawbacks counted for a lot less. On such terrain, heavily armed and armored forces and chariots were cumbersome and unable to move with ease. By contrast, the Israelites' style of warfare was that of nimble guerrillas, able to move fast and take better advantage of whatever opportunities arose to ambush their enemies. Control the Judean mountains, Joshua believed, and the Israelites

Opposite: The ruins of Gezer, the Caananite city that was one of the last to fall into the hands of the Israelites.

would greatly enhance their chances of success.

Joshua's first step toward this goal was to make an alliance with the people of Gibeon (presentday El Jib), a Hivite city some 8 kilometers north of Jerusalem. Like the Israelites, the Gibeonites felt themselves in danger from their more powerful neighbors. The alliance was of strategic value to Joshua, for it secured the Israelite rear and left him free to tackle the problem of Ai, an ancient, heavily fortified town that guarded the Judean heights.

As at Jericho, Joshua sent spies into Ai to scout out the prospects for an attack. Their reports were optimistic. Joshua, encouraged, gathered a force of 3,000 men and began the

Opposite: Joshua led the Israelites through the Caananite territories, his troops made up mostly of light infantry using guerrilla tactics.

assault, but a nasty surprise awaited them.

The defences of Ai were much stronger than the scouts had realized and the defenders a great deal more determined. The result was defeat for Joshua and the Israelites.

Psychologically, it was a severe blow, for Joshua's success this far had created a sense of invincibility for the Israelites. But just as Napoleon Bonaparte said thousands of years later: "A great commander proves his mettle in adversity," Joshua rose to the disappointing occasion in precisely this fashion.

Joshua decided to renew the attack at once, giving the Aians no time for self-congratulation and so catching them off guard. This was not simply an empty flourish of defiance on Joshua's part. He

Hebrew Settlement of Canaan

Early Hebrew settlements

Battles

Conquered cities

Tyre

Laish
(Leshem)

Kedesh

Madon

Achzib

Lake Huleh

Beth-shemesh

Hazor

Acco

Rehob

Chinnereth

Kabul

*Sea of
Chinnereth*

Aphek

Achshaph

Ashtaroth

G r e a t   S e a

Shimron

Yarmuk

Dor

Jokneam

W e s t e r n   S e a

Megiddo

Edrei

Jezreel

Remeth

Kamon

Taanach

Beth-shan

Ham

Ramoth-gilead

Hepher

Ibleam

Jabesh-gilead

P l a i n

Socoh

Jordan

Tirzah

Zaphon

of

Shechem

Succoth

Jabbok

Penuel

S h a r o n

Tappuah

Joppa

Gilgal

Shiloh

Adam

C

Jogbehah

Bethel

Ai

Jazer

Shaalbim

Jericho

Rabbah

Gezer

Aijalon

Gibeon

Ashdod

Ekron

Beth-shemesh

Jerusalem

Abel-keramim

(Jebus)

Beth-jeshimoth

Heshbon

Ashkelon

S h e p h e l a h

Gath?

Jarmuth

Bethlehem

Medeba

P H I L I S T I A

Adullam

*Salt Sea
(Dead Sea)*

Libnah

Gaza

Eglon

Lachish

Hebron

Dibon

Debir

Aroer

Gerar

Goshen

Arnon

Eshtemoa

Beer-sheba

Hormah

Arad?

Kir-hareseth

N e g e v

10 km

10 miles

*Above: The Israelites first settled in the marginal
land of Canaan, before capturing the cities.*

had formed a plan based on guile and deception that he felt was bound to work.

Firstly, Joshua planned to deploy the entire force of Israelites. Next, the main Israelite force would deliberately "lose" the action by trying to mount a frontal attack and then running away, as if they were discouraged. However, what they were actually doing was luring the defenders of Ai out of their city and straight into the arms – in more ways than one – of crack troops specially picked by Joshua for the task.

Once the Aians had left their city without a force to defend it, the rest of the Israelites would move in, take over, and set the city on fire. This would have the effect of trapping the Aians between the main force of the Israelites and the crack troops who had led them away from the city.

Joshua's battle plan worked perfectly, and the upshot was that the defenders of Ai were attacked from both the front and the rear, and in this way were overwhelmed by the Israelite forces. It was later said that not a man among them escaped alive.

Joshua's three great victories, at Jericho, Merom Waters, and Ai, gave the Israelites control over most of Canaan, including the Judean mountains and the plain of Jordan.

To cement that dominance, they concluded alliances with other city-states in the area but destroyed those which refused to cooperate. None of this, however, assured the Israelites untroubled tenure of the Promised Land, for many more wars and battles lay ahead.

The Wars of the Judges

In ancient Israel, the Judges were primarily military leaders but performed the advisory and legal functions of "elders". In the Bible, the Book of Judges names 12 successive leaders who guided the Israelites after the death of Joshua, although 15 are sometimes listed. Several Judges fought battles to ensure that the one-time wanderers in the Sinai Desert became a people with a permanent home of their own. But they had many enemies to overcome among the other tribes in the area, and the struggle was long and hard.

The first of the Judges, Othniel, came to the rescue of the Israelites in around 1227BC, after they had been oppressed for eight years by an enemy known only as Cushan-risathaim, or Cushan of the Double Wickedness. This Cushan may have been an Edomite or a king of Syria, and his defeat by Othniel appears to have been decisive in giving the Israelites a welcome period of peace for the rest of his 40-year tenure.

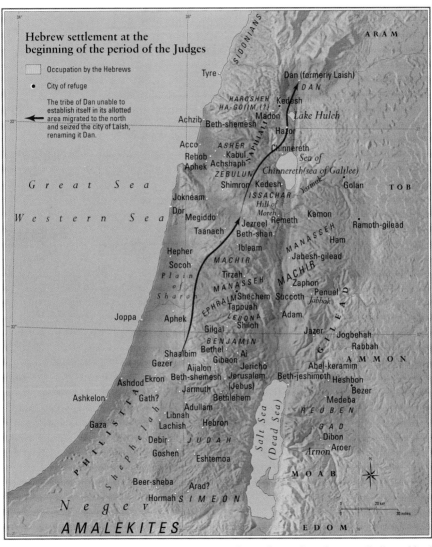

Hebrew settlement at the beginning of the period of the Judges

Occupation by the Hebrews

● City of refuge

The tribe of Dan unable to establish itself in its allotted area migrated to the north and seized the city of Laish, renaming it Dan.

34°   35°

A R A M

SIDONIANS

Tyre

Dan (formerly Laish)

D A N

HAROSHEH HA-GOIIM (?)   Kedesh

Achzib   Beth-shemesh   Madon   *Lake Huleh*

Acco   *ASHER*   Hazor

Rehob   Kabul   Chinnereth

Aphek   Achshaph   *Sea of*

ZEBULUN   *Chinnereth(sea of Galilee)*

Shimron   Kedesh   Golan   T O B

Jokneam   *ISSACHAR*

Dor   Hill of Moreh

Megiddo   Jezreel   Remeth   Kamon

Taanach   Beth-shan   Ramoth-gilead

Hepher   Ibleam   *MANASSEH*   Ham

Socoh   *MACHIR*   Jabesh-gilead

Plain   Tirzah   *MACHIR*

of   *MANASSEH*   Zaphon

Sharon   *EPHRAIM*   Shechem   Succoth   Penuel

Joppa   Aphek   *LEBONA*   Tappuah   *Jabbok*

Shiloh   Adam

Gilgal   Jazer   Jogbehah

BENJAMIN   Rabbah

Shaalbim   Bethel   Ai   A M M O N

Gezer   Aijalon   Gibeon   Jericho   Abel-keramim

Ashdod   Ekron   Beth-shemesh   Jerusalem   Beth-jeshimoth   Heshbon

Ashkelon   Gath?   Jarmuth   (Jebus)   Bezer

Adullam   Bethlehem   Medeba

Gaza   Libnah   *REUBEN*

Lachish   Hebron

Debir   *JUDAH*   *GAD*

Goshen   Dibon

Eshtemoa   *Arnon*   Aroer

PHILISTIA   *Shephelah*

Beer-sheba   M O A B

Hormah   Arad?   *S I M E O N*

N e g e v

AMALEKITES   E D O M

G r e a t   S e a

W e s t e r n   S e a

Salt Sea (Dead Sea)

Above: The Israelite tribes were all allocated land by Joshua, though not all of them completed the conquest of their alloted areas.

But the Promised Land was never a place of peace for very long. After Othniel died, the Israelites fell foul of the Moabites, who were nomads living in the mountains alongside the eastern shore of the Dead Sea. The Moabites, like other nomads in the region – the Ammonites and Amalekites – were inveterate

Below: One of the most famous Judges was Samson, whose strength lay in his hair, which was cut off by a handmaiden on the orders of the traitorous Delilah.

raiders. They were also skillful warriors and held the Israelites in thrall for 18 years after the Moabite king, Eglon, defeated them and set himself up in the city of Jericho.

At length, though, the second Judge, Ehud, who succeeded Othniel in around 1187BC, effected another rescue, by devising a speedy way to end Moabite oppression. If he were to assassinate King Eglon, he believed, then the Moabites would not be able to function, just as a body without a head would not be able to survive.

To this end, Ehud forged a special weapon for the purpose: a short, double-edged sword, about half a meter in length, which he strapped to his right thigh under his clothing. Meanwhile, Ehud stationed Israelite soldiers on the slopes of Mount Ephraim. Then Ehud went to the king's palace

Above: Jepthath vowed to kill the first living thing he laid eyes upon in return for victory against the Ammonites – unfortunately it was his daughter.

in Jericho, where he told the guards that he came with a secret message.

The guards searched Ehud for hidden weapons, but missed the sword he was concealing under his clothes. When Ehud came into the presence of King Eglon, he announced that the message he carried came from God. At that, King Eglon stood up as a mark of respect, but this only made it easier for Ehud to draw his sword and stab the king to death. The blow was so powerful that, it appears, the sword and the hilt disappeared into Eglon's overweight body.

Afterward, Ehud was able to escape from the palace and signaled his army on Mount Ephraim to attack. According to the Book of Judges (Chapter

3, Verse 29), 10,000 Moabites were killed in the ensuing battle and their power over Israel was destroyed.

After that, Ehud is said to have ruled the Israelites for 80 years but once he was dead, the Israelites were again in trouble when the Philistines invaded their territory.

Ehud's successor, Shamgar, led a battle to fight them off, apparently killing 600 Philistines with an ox-goad. The next emergency, however, was much more serious. A century and a half previously, after Joshua's victory over King Jabin of Hazor, the Israelites had failed to expel all the Canaanites from the Promised Land. In the 12th century BC, these residual Canaanites lived on the Plain of Esdraelon, which jutted out into Israelite territory, virtually cutting it in half. This enabled the Canaanites, whose king was another Jabin, to wreak their revenge.

For 20 years, they oppressed the Israelites until Deborah, the fourth leader to become a judge, in around 1106BC, rallied her forces to challenge their power. Some of the Israelites were so cowed by the long years of Canaanite tyranny that they declined to answer the call, but enough of them did to make a small army.

Deborah appointed Barak to take command of the Israelite force, which was of necessity inferior to the soldiery that Sisera, the Canaanite commander, was able to muster. Sisera took to the battlefield, on Mount Tabor in the Valley of Jezreel, with a highly trained, well-equipped force of infantry

Opposite: Some refer to Deborah as the mother of Israel because of the song in the Book of Judges that tells of her defeat of Jabin, King of Hazor.

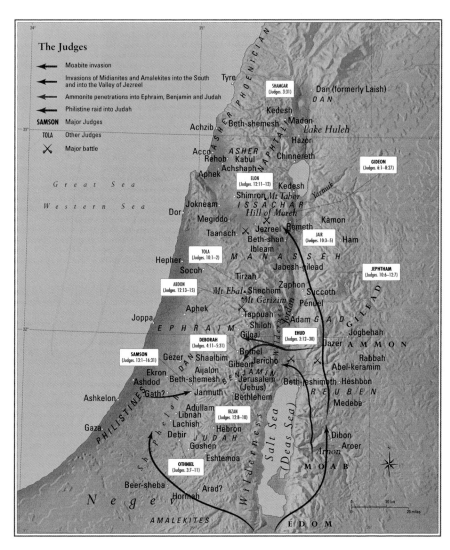

The Judges

← Moabite invasion

← Invasions of Midianites and Amalekites into the South and into the Valley of Jezreel

← Ammonite penetrations into Ephraim, Benjamin and Judah

← Philistine raid into Judah

SAMSON Major Judges

TOLA Other Judges

✕ Major battle

PHOENICIAN

Great Sea

Western Sea

Tyre

SHAMGAR
(Judges 3:31)

Dan (formerly Laish)
DAN

Kedesh

Achzib Beth-shemesh Madon

Acco *ASHER* Chinnereth

Rehob Kabul

Achshaph

Aphek

Lake Huleh

Hazor

ELON
(Judges 12:11–12)

Kedesh

Shimron *Mt Tabor*

ISSACHAR

Jokneam Hill of Moreh

Dor

Megiddo

Taanach Jezreel Remeth

Beth-shan

Ibleam

Kamon

JAIR
(Judges 10:3–5) Ham

GIDEON
(Judges 6:1–8:27)

Yarmuk

NAPHTALI

Hepher

TOLA
(Judges 10:1–2)

MANASSEH

Socoh Jabesh-gilead

Tirzah

Zaphon

JEPHTHAM
(Judges 10:6–12:7)

ABDON
(Judges 12:13–15)

Mt Ebal Shechem

Mt Gerizim Penuel

Succoth

Joppa

Aphek

Tappuah

Adam *GAD*

GILEAD

EPHRAIM

Shiloh

Gilgal

EHUD
(Judges 3:12–30)

Jogbehah

Jazer *AMMON*

DEBORAH
(Judges 4:11–5:31)

Bethel

SAMSON
(Judges 13:1–16:31) Gezer Shaalbim Gibeon Jericho

Ekron Aijalon

Ashdod Beth-shemesh

Gath?

Rabbah

Abel-keramim

BENJAMIN

Jerusalem
(Jebus)

Beth-jeshimoth Heshbon

REUBEN

Medeba

Ashkelon

Jarmuth

Bethlehem

Adullam

Libnah

IBZAN
(Judges 12:8–10)

Lachish

Gaza

Debir *JUDAH*

Hebron

Dibon

Goshen

Eshtemoa

Aroer

Arnon

OTHNIEL
(Judges 3:7–11)

M O A B

*Salt Sea
(Dead Sea)*

Wilderness

Beer-sheba Arad?

Hormah

N e g e v

AMALEKITES *E D O M*

PHILISTINES

20 km

20 miles

*Above: The Book of Judges gives an account
of the attempts each tribe made to conquer their
allotted territories.*

36   Battles of the Bible

and chariots, while the Israelites had no armor and only spears, shields, and a few swords with which to fight.

The odds in favou of the Canaanites looked dauntingly high, until the weather intervened. A cloudburst over Mount Tabor drenched their army and caused the nearby River Kishon to flood. The Canaanite chariots were virtually useless in these conditions and their infantry floundered on the muddy ground.

The Israelites, by contrast, were greatly cheered by the inclement weather, which served to hamper their opponents and equalize the battle. They attacked with the energy of optimism and in the vigorous hand-to-hand fighting that followed, the Canaanite forces began to falter. Sisera was unable to rally them and,

seeing the hopelessness of the situation, he fled.

After their victory on Mount Tabor, the Israelites attacked the plain of Esdraelon, and though they proved unable to conquer all of it, Canaanite power was broken and remained so for another generation.

Unfortunately, history continued to repeat itself, for according to the Book of Judges, victories won and peace restored led inexorably to more sinful behavior and more divine punishment.

This time, it was the Midianites who made life difficult for the Israelites. Like their earlier enemies, the Moabites, the Midianites were nomads, using camels to move quickly across the desert from place to place, raid their victims, and escape with their booty. In attacking the Israelites, the Midianites made a speciality of swooping down at harvest time, destroying or stealing crops, ravaging the land, and afterwards making off at speed toward their camps on the western side of the River Jordan. The Midianites' allies, the Amalekites, compounded this already serious situation in much the same way and, between the two of them, the Israelites became impoverished.

The harvest raiding continued for six years before the fifth Judge, Gideon, whose name meant "destroyer" or "mighty warrior", succeeded to the office in around 1066BC and tackled the problem. According to the Book of Judges, Chapter 6, Verse 16, God told Gideon: "I will be with you, and you will strike down all the Midianites together." What happened next occupies the whole of Chapter 7 in the Book of Judges.

Below: The heavy fortifications of the Canaanite hilltop cities were the last pockets of resistance to fall to the Israelites.

Gideon decided to assault the Midianites not in the conventional fashion, on a field of battle, but where it would hurt them most, at home, in their encampment, where they lived with their families and animals.

Gideon thought this arrangement made it likely that the Midianites could be panicked by a surprise assault. Out of a 32,000-strong army, Gideon kept back 10,000 men as a reserve and, on a dark night in around 1194BC, he gathered a small force of 300 men, divided them into three companies of 100 each, and ordered them to take up positions on three sides of the encampment.

Each man was equipped with a torch, a pottery jar, and a trumpet. The east side of the camp faced rugged terrain and this was left open so that when the Midianites fled, as Gideon was certain they would, they would not find it easy to get away.

When it was dark enough, Gideon gave the signal to attack. Each of his men set his torch flaming, then smashed his jar on the ground, and blew his trumpet. The noise panicked the Midianites and the flaming torches made them fear their tents were about to be set alight. Imagining they were surrounded by a huge enemy force, they fled and in the dark and the confusion set about each other with their swords. Gideon had scored a victory without using a weapon.

But Gideon had not yet finished with the Midianites. As they swarmed away from their encampment in a lather of fear, the 10,000 soldiers of Gideon's reserve set off after them. Many of the Midianites fled without their armor or weapons and the result was a massacre, as the Israelites weighed into the panic-stricken mass and, laying about them with their swords and spears, slew hundreds.

The Israelites did not have it all their own way, though. Gideon's brothers were killed and in revenge for their deaths, he executed the Midianite kings, who were among the prisoners taken. With this, Midianite power in the region was broken.

Gideon remained a judge until his death 40 years later and another 45 years and the 'reigns' of three minor, or non-military, Judges passed before the by-now traditional emergency struck Israel yet again. In around 981 BC, Jephthah, the ninth Judge of Israel, was faced with danger presented by the aggressive Ammonites.

The Ammonites, who lived to the northeast of the Dead Sea, had been enemies of the Israelites as far back as their exodus from Ancient Egypt. The enmity continued after the era of the Judges and on into the reigns of the first two kings of Israel, Saul and David. Nevertheless, in the account of his campaign in the Book of Judges, Jephthah gave the Ammonites a severe beating. He struck at Aroer, on the north bank of the River Amon in present-day Jordan, at Minnith, east of the Jordan river and smashed twenty more cities "with very great slaughter." Thus, the Book of Judges continues: "the children of Ammon were subdued before the children of Israel."

Jephthah was the last of the 12 Judges to go to war in defence of the Israelites, but the biblical book dealing with their exploits has another tale of battle to tell. The last conflict recorded in the Book of Judges took place at Gibeah, three kilometers north of Jerusalem, where two of the tribes of Israel, Levi and Benjamin, clashed in civil strife. The argument that led to the conflict occurred after a mob from Gibeah, a Benjaminite city, killed a concubine belonging to a man from the tribe of Levi. Gibeah was strongly fortified and surrounded by a thick, high wall, which foiled the Levi's first attempts to capture it. At this, the Levi resorted to a cunning ploy. They left their assault troops outside the city and retreated to an area out of sight of the inhabitants, where they set the ambush. When all was ready, the assault force pretended to pull out, persuading the Benjaminites they were giving up and fleeing the scene. The Benjaminites fell for the ruse and rushed out in pursuit. Gibeah was now defenceless. The forces of Levi, lying in ambush, headed for the city and set it alight. When the "fleeing" assault force saw smoke rising from the flames, they turned on their pursuers and the Benjaminites ran into a fierce attack. In the aftermath, scores of Benjaminites were killed, so greatly reducing their number that they were afterwards called "the smallest of all the tribes of Israel."

In the list of 15, rather than 12, Judges of Israel, the last-named was the prophet Samuel, who masterminded the transfer of power to a new type of ruler, as demanded by the Israelites and, it appears, reluctantly conceded by God: the first of the Kings of Israel, Saul. But as things turned out, Saul was not a happy choice.

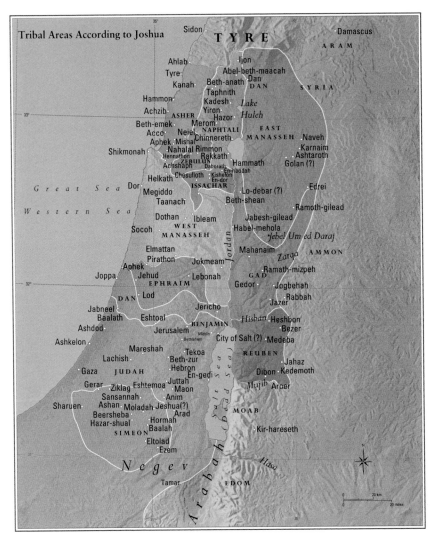

Tribal Areas According to Joshua

Sidon

TYRE

Damascus

ARAM

Ahlab
Tyre
Kanah
Hammon
Achzib
Beth-emek
Acco
Aphek Mishal
Shikmonah

Ijon
Abel-beth-maacah
Beth-anath Dan
Taphnith DAN
Kadesh
Yiron
Hazor
Merom
Neiel Chinnereth

SYRIA

Lake
Huleh

ASHER
NAPHTALI
EAST
MANASSEH Naveh
Karnaim
Nahalal Rimmon Ashtaroth
Hennathon Rakkath Hammath Golan (?)
Achshaph ZEBULUN Daberath
Chesulloth En-haddah Kishion
Helkath En-dor
ISSACHAR
Dor
Megiddo Lo-debar (?) Edrei
Taanach Beth-shean
Dothan Ibleam Ramoth-gilead
Socoh Jabesh-gilead
WEST Habel-mehola
MANASSEH Jebel Um ed Daraj
Elmattan Mahanaim
Pirathon Zarqa AMMON
Aphek Jokmeam
Joppa Jehud Lebonah Ramath-mizpeh
EPHRAIM GAD
Gedor Jogbehah
Lod Jazer Rabbah
Jabneel Jericho
Baalath Eshtoal Hisban Heshbon
Ashdod BENJAMIN Bezer
Jerusalem Middin
Ashkelon Bethlehem City of Salt (?) Medeba
Mareshah Tekoa
Lachish Beth-zur REUBEN Jahaz
Gaza JUDAH Hebron Dibon Kedemoth
Gerar En-gedi
Ziklag Eshtemoa Juttah Mujib Aroer
Sansannah Maon
Sharuen Ashan Anim MOAB
Beersheba Moladah Jeshua(?)
Hazar-shual Hormon Arad Kir-hareseth
SIMEON Baalah
Eltolad
Ezem

Great Sea Dor
Western Sea
Jordan
DAN
Salt Sea (Dead Sea)
Arabah
Negev
Tamar EDOM
Hasa

20 km
20 miles

N

*Above: The Israelites may have controlled less
land at the time of Samuel than they had at the
time of Joshua's death.*

The Wars of the Judges   43

Loss of the Ark

The Ark of the Covenant, which contained the tablets inscribed with the Ten Commandments, was the Israelites' most precious possession. It was regarded as so holy that simply to gaze at it merited punishment. To touch it was punishable by death. The presence of the Ark was also thought to denote God's protection and to assure success: this is why the Ark was carried into battle as the Israelites fought other tribes to carve out the territory of the Promised Land, which they believed that God had granted them.

In practical terms, the risks the Ark ran in these circumstances were considerable and, at the second Battle of Eben-ezer against the Philistines, where 30,000 Israelites were killed, the worst happened.

The Philistines had become the dominant force along the coastline of the Mediterranean during the last days of the Judges. The emnity between these tribes and the Israelites had been growing; the Israelites in fact lived in the hills because of the Philistines' iron chariots, which gave them mobility in the lowlands. At the Battle of Eben-ezer, the two forces fought a pitched battle for the first time.

The Ark was lost, as the Philistines captured it and took it back to the temple of Dagon, their "fish-god." The messenger who carried the dire news to

Shiloh, the religious capital of Israel in the hill country of Ephraim, tore his clothes as a sign of mourning and poured earth on his head. The shock caused by the loss of the Ark was so great that the venerable priest Eli collapsed and died when he learned of it. Eli's daughter-in-law, who gave birth to a son at this time, named the child Ichabod to reflect the disaster: Ichabod meant "Where is glory?"

But according to the first Book of Samuel, the Philistines lived to rue the day they ever laid hands on the Ark. Wherever they carried it, misfortune followed. When the Ark was placed in the temple of Dagon at Ashdod, the idol

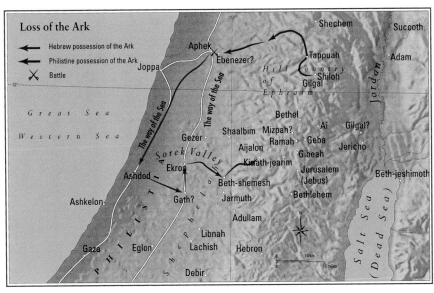

Above: The Israelites took the Ark into battle after their first defeat at Aphek; they were defeated again and the Ark was lost.

Above: The Israelites established a special central sanctuary in the centre of Canaan to house their mobile shrine, the Ark of the Covenant.

of the fish god was later found flat on its face in an attitude of homage. Although placed upright again, the idol was found in the same position next day. The people of Ashdod suffered disease and a plague of mice. Boils afflicted the inhabitants of Gath and Ekron when the Ark was taken there.

Seven months after they captured the Ark, the Philistines had had enough. They consulted their priests, who told them that misfortune would end only if the Ark were restored to the Israelites.

The Philistines were so anxious to get rid of this bringer of misfortune that they offered not only to return the Ark but, in addition, to give the Israelites a coffer full of golden jewels as compensation. The Ark was placed on a cart and taken to Bethshemesh in Judah, where it was greeted with celebratory sacrifices and burnt offerings. But some of the Bethshemites made a bad mistake: out of sheer curiosity, they stared at the Ark. Verse 19, Chapter 6 of the first Book of Samuel described what happened next:

"And he smote the men of Bethshemesh, because they had looked into the Ark of the Lord, even He smote of the people fifty thousand and threescore and ten men: and the people lamented, because the Lord had smitten many of the people with a great slaughter."

Above: The Ark was taken to Kiriath-jearim, where it remained for the next 20 years until David took it to his new capital of Jerusalem.

The Conquests of King Saul

Saul the Benjaminite was chosen as the first King of Israel by the prophet Samuel. A skilled and successful general, Saul spent almost his entire reign fighting against Israel's enemies: the Amalakites and other nomads but most particularly the Philistines, who in the end contrived his downfall and death.

Ever since they arrived in the Promised Land, the Israelites had been obliged to accept as a fact of life the need to fight for their freedom and independence against the many longer-established tribes. Joshua and many of the Judges had been familiar with this syndrome, but it was Saul who had to face the Philistines in the mid-11th century BC, at a time when they were at the apex of their military power.

The basis of Philistine superiority lay in the technology that enabled them to deploy iron weapons, in particular the iron chariot, a shock weapon that appeared suddenly on the battlefield, carrying up to five heavily armed and armored warriors. They would strike

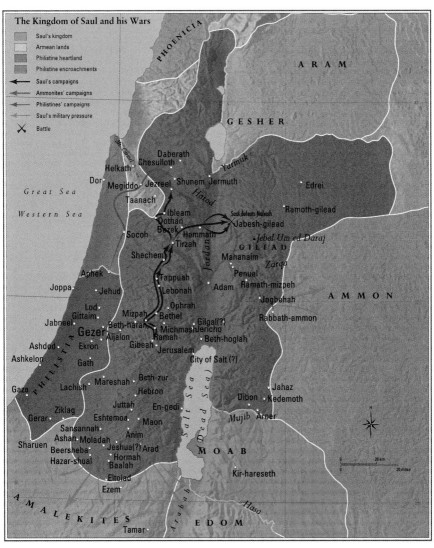

The Kingdom of Saul and his Wars

- Saul's kingdom
- Armean lands
- Philistine heartland
- Philistine encroachments
- Saul's campaigns
- Ammonites' campaigns
- Philistines' campaigns
- Saul's military pressure
- Battle

*Above: The Philistines attempted to expand
their land and contain their enemies, but only
succeeded in uniting them under a single leader.*

The Battles of King Saul 49

hard then speed away before an effective defense could be organized. The Philistines excelled in this context because they were master ironsmiths and saw to it that they retained a virtual monopoly of iron manufacture.

The Israelites, by contrast, were crudely armed, usually with agricultural implements, as the first Book of Samuel (Chapter 13, Verses 19-20) explains: "Now there was no smith found throughout all the land of Israel: for the Philistines said, Lest the Hebrews make them swords or spears: But all the Israelites went down... to sharpen every man his (plough) share, and his coulter, and his axe, and his mattock."

It was with these warriors, thus armed, that King Saul scored his first success in battle, when he relieved the Ammonite siege of Jabesh-Gilead. The siege had continued for so long that the defenders were wilting under the strain and thought about surrendering. But Saul would have none of it. If the King of Ammon, Nahash, were to control Jabesh-Gilead, it meant a hostile intruder planted inside Israelite territory. This, Saul decided, could not be allowed to happen. The problem was that the tribes of Israel were not keen to follow Saul to the rescue. So Saul shocked them into compliance.

"He took a yoke of oxen," the Book of Samuel (Chapter 11, Verse 7) recounts, "and hewed them in pieces and sent them throughout... Israel... saying Whosoever cometh not forth... so shall it be done unto his oxen."

Saul, who was a farmer, knew the dread import of his threat: he was effectively promising the Israelites economic disaster, for the success of farming relied heavily on oxen. Saul's ploy worked. His threat is said to have produced 330,000, men, who presented themselves at Bezek, in the mountains near Jerusalem.

The army of Israel in the 11th century BC was relatively unsophisticated and operated more like guerrilla fighters. Their tactics were no less effective for being unorthodox, as Joshua and the warrior Judges had already proved. They marched by night, surprising their opponents by appearing unexpectedly and approaching swiftly. Their commanders divided their forces and committed them to action in sequence rather than in a big, concerted "push." A reserve of troops was held back so that it could step in with support wherever the front-line troops became too hard-pressed. With these tactics, King Saul was able to relieve the siege of Jabesh-Gilead, but he could not rest on his laurels, for the action had taught him some valuable lessons.

It was evident to Saul that a civilian force that disbanded and went home when the fighting was over was not likely to succeed too often against the professional troops fielded by Israel's Ammonite and other opponents. What was needed was a regular armed force, constantly in training and available at any time for speedy action as and when the king required. Saul resolved to form a standing army, choosing at first a nucleus of 3,000 men that would be permanently on call. As an ancillary to this larger force, Saul created another, smaller army, 1,000-strong, commanded by his son Jonathan, which subsequently

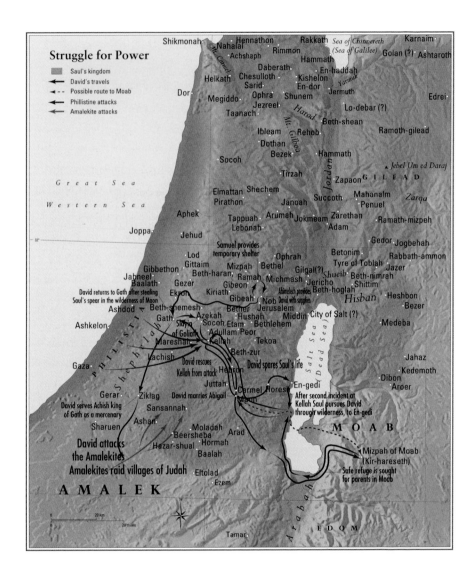

Struggle for Power

- ▢ Saul's kingdom
- ◂— David's travels
- ◂- - Possible route to Moab
- ◂— Phillistine attacks
- ◂— Amalekite attacks

Shikmonah · Nahalal · Hennathon · Rakkath · *Sea of Chinnereth* · Karnaim
Achshaph · Rimmon · *(Sea of Galilee)* · Golan (?) · Ashtaroth
Daberath · En-haddah
Helkath · Chesulloth · Kishelon · Hammath
Sarid · En-dor · *Yarmuk*
Dor · Megiddo · Ophra · Shunem · Jermuth · Edrei
Jezreel · Lo-debar (?)
Taanach · *Harod* · Beth-shean · *Mt. Gilboa*
Ibleam · Rehob · Ramoth-gilead
Dothan
Bezek · Hammath
Socoh · Tirzah · ▲ *Jebel Um ed Daraj*
Zapaon · GILEAD
Great Sea · Elmattan · Shechem
Western Sea · Pirathon · Janoah · Succoth · Mahanalm · *Zarqa*
Aphek · Tappuah · Arumah · Jokmeam · Zarethan · Penuel
Lebonah · Adam · Ramath-mizpeh
Joppa · Jehud
Samuel provides · Gedor · Jogbehah
Lod · temporary shelter · Ophrah · Betonim · Rabbath-ammon
Gibbethon · Gittaim · Mizpah · Bethel · Gilgal(?) · Tyre of Toblah · Jazer
Jabneel · Beth-haran · Ramah · Michmash · *Shueib* · Beth-nimrah
Baalath · Gezer · Gibeon · Jericho · Beth-hoglah · Shittim · Heshbon
David returns to Gath after stealing · Ekron · Kiriath · Ahimelech provides · Beth-hoglah
Saul's spear in the wilderness of Maon · Gibeah · Nob · David with supplies · *Hisban* · Bezer
Ashdod · Beth-shemesh · Bether · Jerusalem
Gath · Azekah · Hushah · Middin · City of Salt (?)
Ashkelon · Socoh · Etam · Bethlehem · Medeba
Slaying · Adullam · Peor
of Goliath · Mareshah · Keilah · Tekoa
Kachish · Beth-zur · Jahaz
Gaza · David rescues · David spares Saul's life · Kedemoth
Lachish · Keilah from attack · Hebron · En-gedi · Dibon
Juttah · Aroer
Gerar · Ziklag · David marries Abigail · Carmel · Horesh
David serves Achish king · Sansannah · After second incident at · M O A B
of Gath as a mercenary · Ashan · Keilah Saul pursues David
Sharuen · through wilderness, to En-gedi
David attacks · Moladah · Arad
the Amalekites · Hazar-shual · Hormah · Mizpah of Moab
Beersheba · (Kir-hareseth)
Amalekites raid villages of Judah · Baalah · Eltolad · Safe refuge is sought
Ezem · for parents in Moab
A M A L E K
Arabah
Tamar · E D O M

0   20 km
0   20 miles

*Above: Saul did not hve the loyalty of the southern
tribes and struggled to maintain his control.*

conquered the Benjaminite city of Gibeah and trounced the Philistine garrison guarding it.

Jonathan's exploit at Gibeah, his father's "home town," struck a crucial blow at Philistine plans to dominate the area. To stunt this enterprise, the Philistines gathered a large force that probably included chariot and cavalry corps and headed for the Bethhoron pass, which ran through the mountains near Jerusalem. There they set up a heavily fortified base at Michmash, on the eastern side of the Judean plateau.

These Philistine moves hit hard at Israelite morale and so many recruits deserted that Saul had only around 600 men to take up position opposite Michmash. The Philistine forces were also depleted, but by design rather than ill fortune: the Philistines had decided to reduce the area on the central plateau by sending three "flying" columns to carry out devastating raids. Although enemy power had been lessened by this extra task, Saul shrank from attacking the Philistines and instead moved his forces to Migron, which was sited opposite Michmash. The Philistines had foreseen this, and set up a "blocking" force of around 20 men at Michmash Pass to keep an eye out for any hostile Israelite moves.

At this juncture, the initiative passed to Saul's son Jonathan, who decided on an audacious and novel strategem which, he hoped, would discombobulate the Philistines. With his shield-bearer, Jonathan made a wide detour to the south. Although they were in full view, the Philistine "blocking" force assumed that they were just traveling through the mountains on some private business of their own and had nothing to do with the Israelite army. The Philistines returned to watching the Israelites for signs of impending action.

Jonathan and his shield-bearer reached Wadi Suweinit, a deep gorge in the mountains and worked their way around until they were close to the cliff near the Philistine positions. The two men climbed the cliff as silently as they could and managed to reach the top unsuspected. The Philistines were completely taken by surprise when they were unexpectedly assaulted from the rear. Jonathan and his shield-bearer were able to kill several of them and the rest, it seemed, took fright and fled.

The effect of this two-man assault was to startle the garrison at Michmash and to persuade them that the Philistines fleeing toward them were an Israelite force charging their positions. Confusion and chaos ensued and Saul, seeing what was happening, took the opportunity to mount a frontal attack on Michmash. The Philistines, already in panic-stricken disarray, broke ranks almost at once and fled the scene.

What they did not know was that their escape route took them past Israelite refugees from the central plateau who had taken shelter in the mountains from the "flying" columns that had devastated their homes and farms. It was not an opportunity to be missed. The refugees fell upon the Philistines so savagely that more of them were killed than had been lost in battle.

This freed Saul from the

Opposite: Saul initially encouraged David, the future king, who was his favorite but was later to become his bitter rival.

attention of his most dangerous enemies and led to a run of success against others, described in the First Book of Samuel (Chapter 14, Verse 47): "So Saul took the kingdom over Israel, and fought against all his enemies on every side, against Moab, and against the children of Ammon, and against Edom, and against the kings of Zobah, and against the Philistines: and whithersoever he turned himself, he vexed them."

Saul's next task was to set up a system of constant patrolling and guarding of the Israelite

Above: Even in his youth, during Saul's reign, David was gaining a formidable reputation.

farming land that was so vulnerable to attack from the Amalekites and other nomads in the Negev Desert. The defense had to be continuous, and eventually led to the building of a line of fortifications along

Opposite: Saul encouraged the clash between David and Goliath, as shown in this painting by Philippe le Bel de Breviare.

Above: Saul's jealousy of David's popularity with the Israelites caused him to flee to the desert region of Judah for safety.

the edge of the desert. The Israelites also set up a series

of fortified camps in the valley that served not only as bases for their campaigns but also as barriers to the Philistines advancing into the mountains.

It was in this context that the famous confrontation took place between the young David and the giant Philistine Goliath. The Israelites, led by Saul, were confronting the Philistines at Socoh in Judah. But there was no fighting, only a 40-day stand-off during which the Philistines sent their strongman, Goliath, twice a day, to demand that Saul provide a champion to settle the matter in single combat. Goliath was 6 feet 7 inches tall and, at first, there was no one willing to take him on. Saul, growing desperate, offered a reward to anyonr who would defeat and kill the giant. No one volunteered until David offered to take up the challenge. Saul was doubtful, but offered David

Above: Saul, unable to face the humiliation of
defeat at Gibeon, threw himself on his own sword.

his armor, helmet, and sword. Physically, the youth was far too small to wear any of it, and instead went out to confront Goliath armed only with a sling and five round stones taken from the nearby brook. David used his sling to fling one of his stones and hit the target at once, striking the giant squarely on the forehead. Goliath fell flat on his face, unconscious. David rushed forward, seized Goliath's sword and cut off his head. The Philistine army, shocked at this outcome, fled in disarray.

However, the demoralizing effect of David's unexpected triumph and King Saul's efforts to keep the Philistines at bay did not entirely dissipate the threat they represented. After the battle of Michmash, the Philistines made several attempts to get at the central mountain massif from the west, but all failed. A new approach was required, and the Philistines planned to surround Ir-ganim (present-day Jenin) by marching north across the coastal plain, the Plain of Sharon, through a pass in the Carmel mountain range into the Valley of Jezreel. This would enable them to move south along the plateau.

Saul had effective spies and was able to watch the Philistines with a view to seeing which direction they took. That done, he paralleled their forces with his own to block the Philistines' ascent to Ir-ganim in the foothills of the Gilboa range of mountains. But success was not going to be easy and Saul grew nervous when he saw how immense the opposing army was. The Philistines had brought some 6,000 cavalry and 30,000 chariots for what was to be Saul's last battle. The pressure this immense

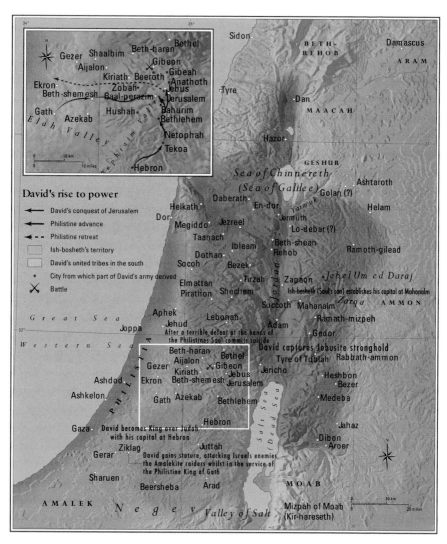

Above: The Philistine army, with David in its service, marched against Saul and met him at Geibeon, where he was defeated.

force exerted obliged Saul to retreat up Mount Gilboa. The Philistine chariots, with their cargo of archers, followed him. When Saul and his pursuers reached the flat plateau at the top, the archers loosed a storm of arrows to which the Israelites had no effective answer.

It was a massacre and Saul was soon convinced that defeat and, consequently, his capture were inevitable. Unable to face the humiliation and disgrace, he killed himself by falling on his sword. Jonathan, his son, died in the fighting. The consternation among the Israelites was extreme, and it fell to David, now a grown man and the next leader of Israel, to lament the lost king and his valiant son in his elegy: "The beauty of Israel is slain upon the high places. How are the mighty fallen! Tell it not in Gath, publish it not in the streets of Askelon; lest the daughters of the Philistines rejoice... Ye mountains of Gilboa, let there be no dew, neither let there be rain, upon you, nor fields of offerings... Saul and Jonathan were lovely and pleasant in their lives, and in their death they were not divided: they were swifter than eagles, they were stronger than lions. How are the mighty fallen, and the weapons of war perished!"

The reign of David, who succeeded Saul, is regarded as a golden age in which he turned Saul's kingdom into a far-flung empire. The one-time boy shepherd in Bethlehem, later King Saul's court musician, began his reign by capturing Jerusalem, fortifying it and building himself a palace. The Philistines felt their power was in danger, and went to war. David, undaunted, hit back...

The Wars of King David

David was initially elected King of Judah in around 1007BC, with Saul's eldest surviving son, Ishbosheth, ruling over the rest of Israel. Before David became king of united Israel (Israel and Judah) after the assassination of Ishbosheth seven years later, he had some unfinished business to settle: control of the Negev nomads, who were making constant and damaging inroads into Judean territory.

Keeping the nomads out of Judah, where settlements in the Hebron mountains were in the front line of their attacks, could not be dealt with by a single, decisive battle – it had to be a long-term strategy. Fortunately, Saul had already done the groundwork for an army capable of doing the job properly, and David was able to call on highly trained, battle-hardened soldiers whom he settled, with their families, among the Hebronite communities. Their task was to guard the settlements and lead local forces against the desert raiders whenever they appeared. David, however, also envisaged a larger canvas

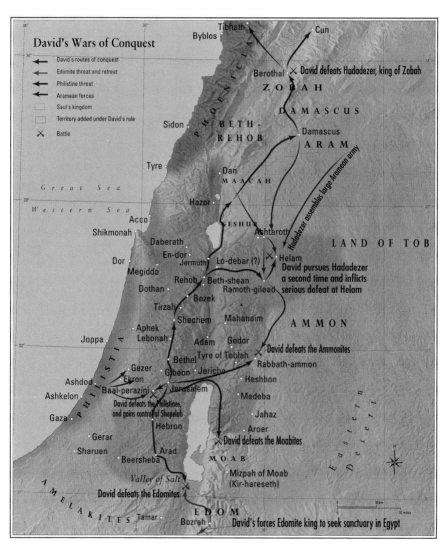

David's Wars of Conquest

- ← David's routes of conquest
- ← Edomite threat and retreat
- ← Philistine threat
- ← Aramean forces
- ☐ Saul's kingdom
- ☐ Territory added under David's rule
- ✗ Battle

Tibhath
Byblos
Cun
Berothai ✗ David defeats Hadadezer, king of Zobah
Z O B A H
D A M A S C U S
Sidon
B E T H -
R E H O B
Damascus
A R A M
Tyre
Dan
M A A C A H
Great Sea
Hazor
Western Sea
Acco
GESHUR
Shikmonah
Ashtaroth
L A N D   O F   T O B
Daberath
En-dor
Jermuth
Lo-debar (?)
Helam
Dor
Megiddo
Rehob
Beth-shean
Ramoth-gilead
David pursues Hadadezer
a second time and inflicts
serious defeat at Helam
Dothan
Bezek
Tirzah
Mahanaim
Shechem
A M M O N
Aphek
Joppa
Lebonah
Adam
Gedor
Tyre of Toblah
David defeats the Ammonites
Bethel
Gezer
Gibeon
Jericho
Rabbath-ammon
Ashdod
Ekron
Heshbon
Baal-perazim
Ashkelon
Jerusalem
Medeba
David defeats the Philistines,
and gains control of Shepelah
Gaza
Jahaz
Hebron
Aroer
Gerar
✗ David defeats the Moabites
Sharuen
Arad
M O A B
Beersheba
Eastern Desert
Valley of Salt
Mizpah of Moab
(Kir-hareseth)
David defeats the Edomites
A M A L E K I T E S
Tamar
E D O M
Bozrah
David's forces Edomite king to seek sanctuary in Egypt

Hadadezer assembles large Aramean army

*Below: King David provided security for his
subjects by defeating the Philistines, establishing
his rule from Damascus to the Egyptian border.*

The Wars of King David   65

Above: The gate traditionally held to be the entrance to David's citadel in his capital city of Jerusalem.

helmets, armor, and large shields.

After David became king of all Israel in around 1000BC, his first task was to acquire a capital and, for this, only one city would do: Jerusalem, centrally placed in the mountains, with access to the Mediterranean and a position commanding the crossroads of the route between the sea and the Jordan River. Jerusalem was also situated in an ideal defensive position on a ridge, with valleys on all four sides. This, of course, was a problem that King David, as a would-be conqueror, had to face when he embarked on his first military campaign against the Jebusites, an "aboriginal" tribe that controlled Jerusalem and the surrounding region.

for his army and one that would have to cater for the military needs of a united Israel. He continued Saul's work in building his army into a fully professional force, which served full-time and trained hard between wars and battles to increase its military expertise.

Instead of the agricultural implements of earlier times, David's soldiers were armed with swords and spears and just as strongly protected by

Jebusite Jerusalem was heavily fortified, but David nevertheless secured a position in the citadel that was situated high up in the northern sector of the ridge. This possessed a significant advantage: a low section of the ridge led to a part of Jerusalem that was later known as the Temple Mount. At this juncture, though, David

and his forces came up against another difficulty: the Jebusites, it seems, had placed the defense of Jerusalem in the hands of "the blind and the lame". This curious phrase denoted something truly fearful at a time when superstition was an awesome force in human affairs: according to one interpretation it meant that a magic spell had been cast over the defenses, and that was enough to deter

Below: David's reign was a golden age in which culture was as important as war – David himself was known for composing psalms.

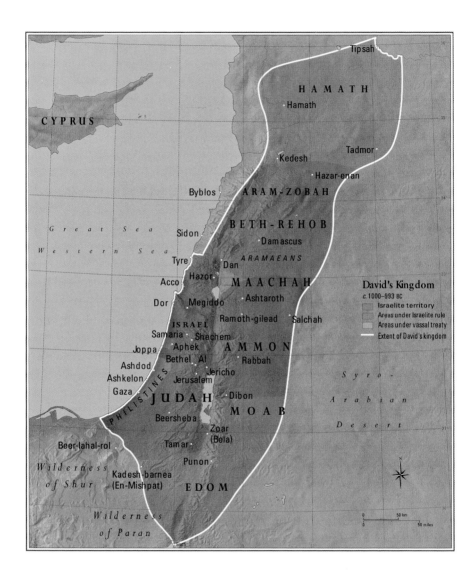

Tipsah

HAMATH

Hamath

CYPRUS

Tadmor

Kedesh

Hazar-enan

Byblos

ARAM-ZOBAH

G r e a t   S e a

Sidon

BETH-REHOB

Damascus

W e s t e r n   S e a

Tyre

A R A M A E A N S

Dan

Acco

Hazor

MAACHAH

Dor

Megiddo

Ashtaroth

David's Kingdom

c. 1000–993 BC

☐ Israelite territory
☐ Areas under Israelite rule
☐ Areas under vassal treaty
— Extent of David's kingdom

ISRAEL

Ramoth-gilead

Salchah

Samaria

Shechem

Joppa

Aphek

AMMON

Ashdod

Bethel Ai

Rabbah

Ashkelon

Jericho

S y r o -

Gaza

Jerusalem

A r a b i a n

JUDAH

Dibon

D e s e r t

Beersheba

MOAB

Beer-lahal-rol

Zoar
(Bela)

Tamar

W i l d e r n e s s

Punon

o f   S h u r

Kadesh-barnea
(En-Mishpat)

EDOM

N

W i l d e r n e s s

0   50 km

o f   P a r a n

0   50 miles

Elath

*Above: David established an empire that extended
a long way past the borders of his core territories.*

David's army from proceeding any further.

Another way had to be found. Surveying the scene around him, David spotted a *tzinor*, a passage hewn out of the rock that led under the city wall, and down the eastern slope of the ridge to the Gihon Spring, the main water source for Jerusalem. David decided to mount an attack through the *tzinor* and so emerge when, and where, the Jebusites least expected him. But the assault required a climb up a vertical shaft over 15 meters high that linked the tunnel itself to the channel through which the waters of Gihon Spring passed.

In addition to a willingness to perform this athletic feat, a deft piece of psychological bribery was going to be necessary to find a leader brave enough to defy the magic spell. As the first Book of Chronicles (Chapter 11, Verse 6) recorded:

"And David said, Whosoever smiteth the Jebusites first shall be chief and captain. So Joab the son of Zeruiah went first up, and was chief."

It can be safely assumed that the Jebusites were shocked and dismayed when Joab and his men suddenly appeared at the entrance to the *tzinor*, so much so that they were unable to prevent them from establishing a foothold inside the city. Meanwhile, David's soldiers rushed in and completed the capture of Jerusalem.

David's success in securing Jerusalem rang alarm bells among the Philistines, who already had painful experience of how effective Israelite warriors could be. Hoping to stem further Israelite advances, the Philistines staged incursions through the Elah Valley, which

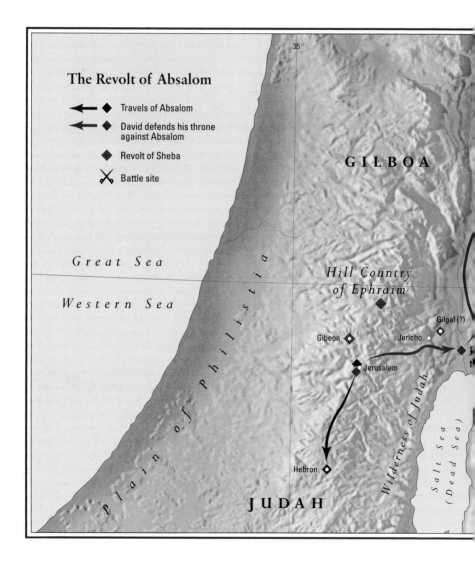

The Revolt of Absalom

⬅◆ Travels of Absalom

⬅◆ David defends his throne against Absalom

◆ Revolt of Sheba

✗ Battle site

Great Sea

Western Sea

Plain of Philistia

GILBOA

Hill Country of Ephraim

Gilgal (?)

Gibeon

Jericho

Jerusalem

Wilderness of Judah

Salt Sea (Dead Sea)

Hebron

JUDAH

35°

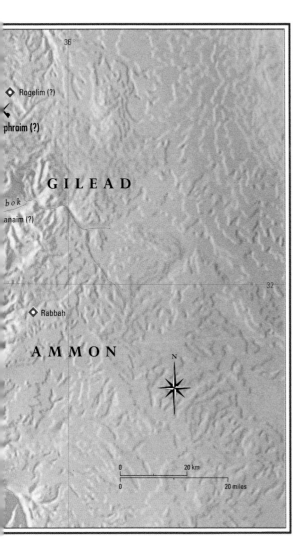

Rogelim (?)

phraim (?)

GILEAD

bok

anaim (?)

Rabbah

AMMON

N

0   20 km
0   20 miles

Left: Toward the end of his reign, David's third son, Absalom, staged a revolt that was defeated. David then named Solomon as his successor.

coincidentally was the scene of the boy David's famous encounter with the giant Goliath.

It appears, though, that, during their first incursion, the Philistines relied too much on the memory of Saul's defeat on Mount Gilboa and seemed to expect a repeat performance from King David. They were wrong.

David bided his time and allowed the Philistines to penetrate deep into the Judean mountains. By the time they reached the Rephaim Valley, west-southwest of Jerusalem, David and his forces had taken up a well-concealed position nearby. The Philistines suddenly found themselves attacked from the rear and fled in panic. So anxious were they to escape that they omitted to take their sacred images with them.

When the Philistines tried again, they once more chose the Rehaim Valley as their way in. Once again, though, they were taken by surprise after the Israelite forces slipped through a forest behind them and emerged from the trees in a fierce assault.

Approaching through woodland ran the risk that the Philistines would hear the Israelites coming, but David nullified any noise with a cunning ploy: knowing that a breeze off the sea reached the Jerusalem area around midday, he timed his attack so that the rustling of the trees muffled the sound of the Israelites' footsteps.

The double defeat in the Valley of Rehaim heralded a determined campaign by David and the Israelites to eliminate the danger the Philistines posed to the peace and security of Israel. To this end, David established a hold over the coastline from the Yarkon River to the Sorek Valley and took over Gath, one of the five Philistine city-states, and the port of Jaffa. However, David never entirely crushed the Philistines, who took every opportunity to attack and harrass the Israelites. They were still at it more than a century after David's death, in the reign of his son King Solomon.

Following Rephaim, David and the Israelites extended their conquests to Trans-Jordan, where they defeated the kingdom of Moab and the Edomites. After that, though, they came up against much more formidable foes. Taken together, the Aramean kingdoms comprised a rich, powerful, technologically advanced network inhabiting

the area to the northeast of the Kingdom of Israel, now known as the Golan Heights. The Arameans entered the wars of King David after Hanun, King of the Ammonites, began to suspect that his realm was David's next target. The Arameans, whose help Hanun enlisted, were themselves worried by David's run of conquests and committed an army some 25,000 strong to the fight.

The Arameans' first assault took place when they came to the aid of the Ammonites at the siege of the fortress of Medeba. An attack from the rear against the Israelite army failed when its commander, Joab, was forewarned by the defense screen he had put in place for just such an eventuality. But Hadadezer, King of Zobah, one of the leading Aramean rulers, resolved to try again and raised an army that included 1,000 chariots, 700 horsemen, and 20,000 foot soldiers.

King David rushed in with his army to do battle with Hadadezer at Helam, in southern Syria. The action was briefly, but vividly, recorded in the second Book of Samuel (Chapter 10, Verses 17-18):

"And the Syrians set themselves in array against David, and fought with him. And the Syrians fled before Israel; and David slew the men

Below: From the foothills of southern Judea, the coastal plains of Philistia, where the Israelites fought their long campaigns, can be seen.

of 700 chariots... and forty thousand horsemen, and smote Shobach the captain of their host, who died there."

By the end of his long reign, David's military exploits had created a vast, rich, powerful empire. His third son, Absalom, attempted to stage a revolt but, after crushing it, David named another of his sons as successor. He died in around 970BC, as the first Book of Chronicles (Chapter 29, Verse 28) put it, "in a good old age, full of days, riches, and honour: and Solomon his son reigned in his stead."

Solomon's Kingdom

Solomon was the son of David, whom he succeeded as King of Israel. During his reign of some 40 years, Solomon came to resemble an eastern potentate with the grandeur of his court, his reportedly extensive harem of wives and concubines, his massive building projects, and lucrative trade links with Phoenicia, Egypt, southern Arabia, Syria, and Cilicia.

Above all, Solomon's triumph was to centralize the government of Israel, concentrating as much of the power as possible in his own hands as king, rather than in that of regional rulers and advisers, and thereby nullifying at least partly the tribal nature of his subjects that had not always been an advantage to his kingdom in the past.

King Solomon is frequently described in superlatives. His wisdom was said to be legendary. His literary skills were such that the biblical Books of Proverbs and Ecclesiastes, as well as the Song of Solomon, have been

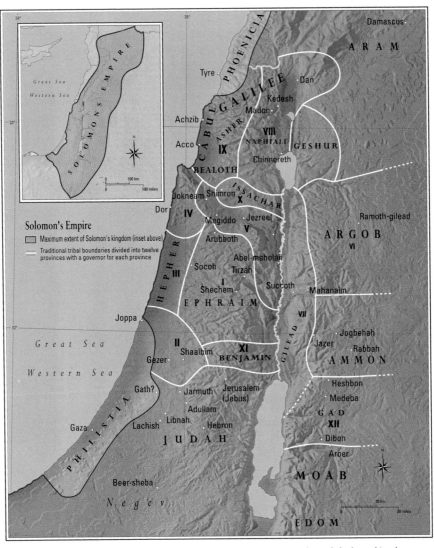

Above: Solomon inherited the large kingdom put together by his father, David, and swiftly eliminated his rivals to ensure his succession.

Above: The great temple built by Solomon stood on the Dome of the Mount in Jerusalem, a place now occupied by an Islamic shrine.

ascribed to him. He was credited with writing 3,000 parables and 1,005 poems. He could discourse with visitors and courtiers about a wide range of subjects, from trees, animals, and birds to insects and fish.

Solomon had been anointed before his father's death, but his first act upon ascending to the throne was to ruthlessly remove any possible rivals, ensuring that he met no challenge in taking over the rulership of the kingdom.

The Bible records Solomon

as a monarch who "ruled over all the kingdoms from the River Euphrates to the land of the Philistines as far as the border of Egypt." His annual income in tributes, which were paid from each of his vassal states, amounted to 666 talents of gold – which is a total of approximately 22,657 kilograms.

Solomon's army is said to have included some 12,000 cavalry and 1,400 chariots. At Megiddo, the remains of 450 stalls for horses have been found during archeological excavations. Solomon's reputed 700 marriages and 300 concubines did not arise solely out of his famous love for women – though that was undoubtedly an important influence, too – but also as a means of cementing political alliances. It was precisely for this reason that he married

Naamah, daughter of the Ancient Egyptian pharaoh Psusennes II, the last ruler of the 21st dynasty.

A special palace of her own, probably sited within Solomon's own palace by the Euphrates river, was specially constucted for Namaan. For the same political purpose, Solomon also married several other women from Moab, Sidon, Ammon, and the land of the Hittites, all of whom were described simply as 'foreign princesses".

Although facilities and teachers were provided for their conversion to Judaism, the fact that Solomon allowed his wives to bring their own shrines for worshipping the pagan gods of their countries spoke of his religious tolerance where these women were concerned.

Like many mighty rulers,

King Solomon was renowned for being a great builder, which enabled him to leave behind plenty of tangible evidence of his reign and its glory.

Solomon's buildings were major projects, sometimes taking many years to complete. Solomon's famous palace, for example, was a work that occupied 13 years and required the recruitment of some 30,000 Israelites as well as a massive army of slaves from among the Amorites, Hittites, Hivites, Jebusites, and Perizzites.

Mesopotamia at that time was frequently a war zone, so an important building project commissioned by Solomon comprised the fortification of the walls of Jerusalem and other strategic towns within his territories such as Hazor, Megiddo, and Tel Gezer.

Excavations carried out in 2006 at Tel Gezer, which lay between present-day Jerusalem and Tel Aviv, revealed a fortification system measuring 40 meters together with a six-chambered gate. Among Solomon's other projects were an extensive ship-building program, water works, cities designed for keeping stores, fortresses situated in the desert, military housing complexes, and vast stables for the army's horses.

But the greatest and most important of all Solomon's many building projects was the temple in the city of Jerusalem, which was also known as the First Temple – the first temple, that is, of the faith of Judaism. The Temple, which took seven years to complete, became the focus of religious observance among the Jewish people, which turned ancient Jerusalem into a place of pilgrimage – and an important commercial center.

The site of Solomon's temple is believed to be the hill that today is known as Temple Mount and lies at the center of the area known as the Dome of the Rock. The likely historical existence of the Temple has been advanced by archaeologists who, in November 1999, unearthed refuse from a very large construction site on Temple Mount. Another discovery, made in the summer of 2007, found "proof of human activity" that could have belonged to the Temple period.

Below: Excavations at Megiddo have revealed the great walls and enormous gateway that were built by King Solomon in order to strengthen Palestine after the Hebrew people captured it. This was one of many building projects undertaken by Solomon that called for high taxes and forced labor, which many in the north of the kingdom resented.

The Temple itself measured 30 cubits, or some 18 meters, in height and was 12 meters in width. Constructed in an oblong shape, it had three "compartments", whose details were variously recorded in the Bible in the books of 1 and 2 Kings, the Book of Hebrews, 2 Chronicles, and the Book of Jeremiah.

The Ulam, which was the porch or entrance, was 12 meters long and six meters deep. Inside the porch, there stood two pillars, each 11 meters tall and each surmounted by capitals in the shape of lilies that were three meters high. The temple floor was made of fir, overlaid in gold, and the olive-wood dorposts supported folding doors of fir.

The Holy of Holies was the inner sanctuary believed to be the dwelling place of God.

It was 12 meters long, wide and high, although these measurements do not take into account the possibility that it stood on a raised floor or cella, as was common for such features in ancient temples.

The floor of the Holy of Holies was made of Cedar of Lebanon, as was the wainscotting. There was gold overlay on both the floor and the walls. In front of the Holy of Holies, there stood a golden altar where incense was burned along with a table for "showbread", which was twelve loaves placed there on every Sabbath and eaten by the priests at the end of the week. The table itself was made of gold, with five candlesticks on each side. Gold was also used for the equipment needed for the candles, such as shuffers, tongs, and fire-pans.

The Hekhal, or holy place,

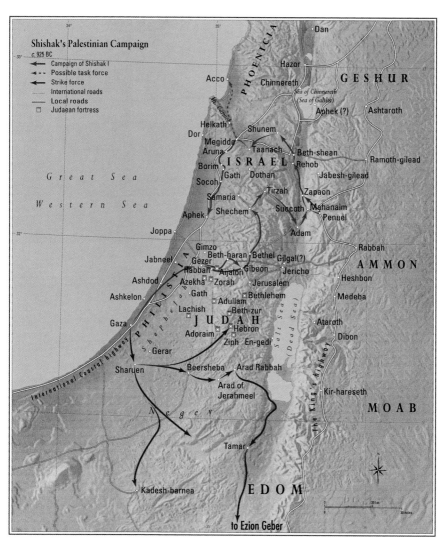

Shishak's Palestinian Campaign

c. 925 BC

- ← Campaign of Shishak I
- ◄ - - Possible task force
- ← Strike force
- International roads
- Local roads
- ⬚ Judaean fortress

Dan

Hazor

Acco

Chinnereth

Sea of Chinnereth (Sea of Galilee)

PHOENICIA

GESHUR

Aphek (?)

Ashtaroth

Helkath

Dor

Shunem

Megiddo

Aruna

Taanach

Beth-shean

Ramoth-gilead

Borim

ISRAEL

Rehob

Socoh

Gath

Dothan

Jabesh-gilead

Samaria

Tirzah

Zapaon

Aphek

Shechem

Succoth

Mahanaim

Penuel

Joppa

Adam

Great Sea

Western Sea

Gimzo

Beth-haran

Bethel

Gilgal(?)

Rabbah

AMMON

Jabneel

Gezer

Rabbah

Ajalon

Gibeon

Jericho

Heshbon

Ashdod

Azekha

Zorah

Jerusalem

Ashkelon

Gath

Bethlehem

Medeba

Adullam

Lachish

Beth-zur

Gaza

JUDAH

Hebron

Ataroth

Adoraim

Ziph

En-gedi

Dibon

Salt Sea (Dead Sea)

Gerar

Sharuen

Beersheba

Arad Rabbah

Kir-hareseth

Arad of Jerahmeel

MOAB

Negev

International Coastal highway

Shephelah lowlands

PHILISTIA

The King's Highway

Tamar

Kadesh-barnea

EDOM

to Ezion Geber

Above: Shishak, or Shoshenq, invaded the Hebrew kingdoms in around 925BC, ending the amicable relations established during Solomon's time.

Solomon's Kingdom 83

Above: The Egyptians were one of the many formidable threats surrounding the Judean empire during Solomon's reign.

was also called the "greater house." Its height and width matched those of the Holy of Holies, but it was 24 meters long. The walls of the Hekhal were lined with cedar which was decorated with carvings of cherubim, palm trees, and flowers overlaid with gold. It was marked off from the Holy of Holies by golden chains.

There were chambers on three sides of the Temple, which were used for storage, and two courts surrounding the building. One was the priests' court or inner court which had a hewn stone wall surmounted by beams of cedar. The priests' court included the Altar, where burnt offerings were made, the

oxen, represented a Mikvah, which gave priests the opportunity to immerse their entire bodies for the purposes of purification. There were, in addition, ten other lavers, each reckoned to contain "40 baths" where worshippers could wash their hands before prayers. These lavers were also of the minimum size for a Mikvah.

The other court of Solomon, which was known as the "great court", ran the whole way around the Temple to accommodate the people who came to worship there.

The jewel in the crown of the Temple was the Ark of the Covenant, the symbol that the Judeans prized over all others and carried with them into war to ensure victory over their enemies. Such a precious item required the utmost protection and when, at last, it

brazen Sea, or laver, made of brass and measuring six meters wide and three meters deep, with an 18 meter circumference. The Book of Kings gives the Sea a capacity of "2,000 baths" (which is the equivalent of 24,000 US gallons) although the Book of Chronicles increases this by half as much again.

The Sea, which was set on the backs of twelve sculptured

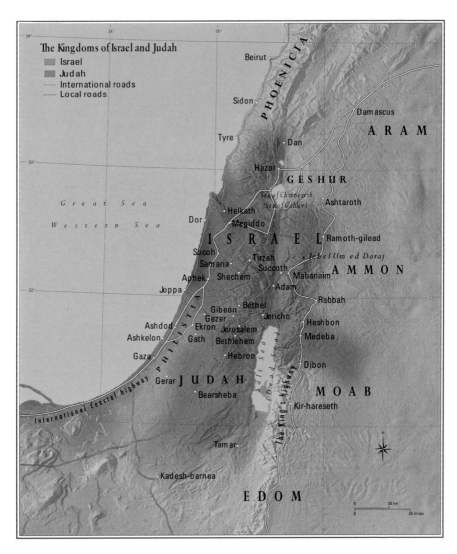

The Kingdoms of Israel and Judah

▨ Israel
▨ Judah
═══ International roads
─── Local roads

Beirut

Sidon

PHOENICIA

Damascus

Tyre

Dan

ARAM

Hazor

GESHUR

Great Sea

Sea of Chinneroth
(Sea of Galilee)

Ashtaroth

Western Sea

Dor

Helkath

Megiddo

ISRAEL

Ramoth-gilead

Socoh

Jebel Um ed Daraj

Samaria

Tirzah

Succoth

AMMON

Aphek

Shechem

Mahanaim

Joppa

Adam

Gibeon

Bethel

Rabbah

Gezer

Jericho

Ashdod

Ekron

Jerusalem

Heshbon

Ashkelon

Gath

Bethlehem

Medeba

Gaza

Hebron

Salt Sea (Dead Sea)

Dibon

Gerar

JUDAH

MOAB

Beersheba

Kir-hareseth

International Coastal highway

The King's highway

PHILISTIA

Tamar

Kadesh-barnea

EDOM

0   30 km
0   30 miles

Above: Solomon succeeded in ruling over a full
Judean kingdom, but after his death it fell into
two pieces: Israel and Judah.

was installed, 22,000 oxen and 120,000 sheep were sacrificed in celebration and a feast lasting 14 days followed.

But Solomon's image of fabulous wealth and dazzling grandeur was not at all easy to create or maintain. For a start, Solomon's right to the throne of Israel was disputed even before he became king.

Solomon was the favorite of his father, King David, partly, it seems, because his mother was Bathsheba, the wife whom David adored and for whose sake he had engineered the death of her first husband, Uriah the Hittite. David's passion for Bathsheba was so intense that he took the ultimate risk: angering God, who took some time to forgive him for his transgressions. But with his 18 wives – apparently the limit placed on the marriages of a Jewish king – David had many

other sons, and to ensure the succession he wanted, he had Solomon anointed by priests in a ceremony at the Spring of Gihon, which was normally reserved for a coronation.

This favoritism aroused the jealousy and fury of Adonijah, Solomon's elder half-brother, who was the son of another of David's 18 wives, Haggith. As David aged and declined, Adonijah resolved that the throne of Israel should be his, despite the preferences of his father.

Adonijah, it seems, was something of a spoiled brat, never disciplined by his father and, being very good looking, somewhat vain. He acquired a force of chariots and recruited some 50 supporters. In his bid to become king, he also enlisted the help of his cousin Joab, the commander of David's army, and Abiathar the priest. But Adonijah's ambitions were blocked by some strong opposition, from Zadok, another priest, Benaiah, son of the priest Jehoiada, who was David's chief bodyguard, and Nathan the prophet, among others. Adonijah, it appears, decided to enlist God's help and sacrificed sheep, oxen, and calves to Him.

King David, it appears, died at around this time, and Adonijah invited the old king's other sons to join him in celebrating his "accession" to the throne of Israel. They all sat down to a great banquet, where they toasted him with shouts of "Long live King Adonijah!"

Unfortunately, the celebrations were not destined to last long. The guests quickly deserted Adonijah when it turned out that Solomon, now king, had learned what his half-brother was doing and summoned him to his presence. Adonijah was utterly terrified of Solomon and expected some heavy punishment, but Solomon dismissed him and told him to go home.

But Solomon's clemency made Adonijah bolder than ever and he demanded that he be allowed to marry Abishag, who had once been a companion to King David. Solomon instantly suspected that this was part of a renewed bid on Adonijah's part to claim the throne. He decided to cut short the attempt, and ordered Adonijah to be executed. Joab was also put to death and the priest Abiathar was exiled.

Solomon was around 18 years of age when he became king of Israel, but he was already canny enough to know how to organize the vast territory he had inherited

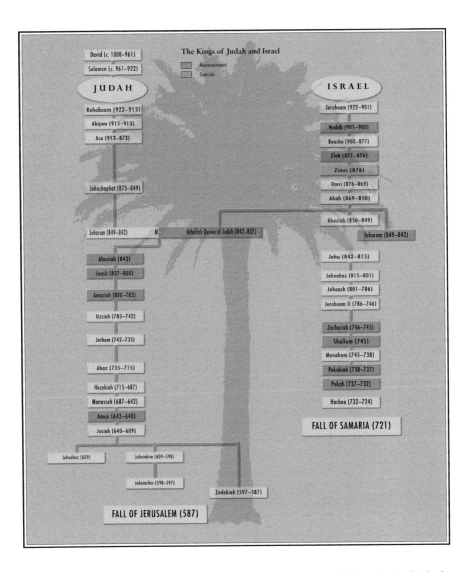

The Kings of Judah and Israel

- ▢ Assassinated
- ▢ Suicide

JUDAH

David (c. 1000–961)
Solomon (c. 961–922)
Rehoboam (922–915)
Abijam (915–913)
Asa (913–873)
Jehoshaphat (873–849)
Jehoram (849–842) M. Athaliah Queen of Judah (842–837)
Ahaziah (842)
Joash (837–800)
Amaziah (800–783)
Uzziah (783–742)
Jotham (742–735)
Ahaz (735–715)
Hezekiah (715–687)
Manasseh (687–642)
Amon (642–640)
Josiah (640–609)
Jehoahaz (609) Jehoiakim (609–598)
Jehoiachin (598–597)
Zedekiah (597–587)

FALL OF JERUSALEM (587)

ISRAEL

Jeroboam (922–901)
Nadab (901–900)
Baasha (900–877)
Elah (877–876)
Zimri (876)
Omri (876–869)
Ahab (869–850)
Ahaziah (850–849)
Jehoram (849–842)
Jehu (842–815)
Jehoahaz (815–801)
Jehoash (801–786)
Jeroboam II (786–746)
Zechariah (746–745)
Shallum (745)
Menahem (745–738)
Pekahiah (738–737)
Pekah (737–732)
Hoshea (732–724)

FALL OF SAMARIA (721)

*Above: Solomon succeeded David; after his death
the line of kings split between Israel and Judah.*

Solomon's Kingdom   89

*Above: Solomon's territories were vast – too
expansive to be easily controlled and defended. He
allowed his grasp on the further reaches to wane
and concentrated on the inner regions.*

from his father. He was unable to hold on to the further reaches of David's empire, such as Damascus in Syria, but he was able to ensure that what he did hold on to, he held on to strongly.

Solomon's method for securing the lands of Israel involved the building of mighty fortresses to protect the land and people, placed in strategic positions at Hazor, Megiddo, Bethhoron, and Baalath.

Hazor guarded the northern frontier of Solomon's realm, while Megiddo kept watch over the plain of Esdraelon. Beth-Horon and Baalath commanded the Valley of Aijalon, which ran from east to west and connected the Coastal Plain to the Judean mountains.

Chariots were, of course, a "must" for any professional army of the time, and Solomon made sure to maintain a large force of them within his own: he even selected Megiddo, which lay south of present day Haifa, as a special chariot city.

In addition to guarding Solomon's northern frontier, Megiddo commanded the eastern approaches of Nahal Iron – "Nahal" meant dry river bed – as well as a section of the international route from Egypt through the coastal plain to the Valley of Jezreel and so on to Damascus and Mesopotamia. The importance of Megiddo – both in Solomon's times and afterward – was highlighted by the number of battles that were fought for control of the fortress.

Megiddo was, in fact, such a frequent battlefield that this may have given rise to the legend that the Tel Megiddo, the hill of Megiddo – which is better known as Armageddon – would be the site of the last battle between good and evil.

Megiddo, however, was not just one city. There were at least 20 cities built on the site during some 5,000 years of continuous habitation. One of these rebuildings was accomplished by Solomon, who made it into a royal center. Solomon's architects provided Megiddo with large palaces and administrative buildings that featured *ashlars*, large, thick walls that were strong enough to support a second story.

Solomon also furnished Megiddo with stables that had perforated stones designed to tie up the horses. There was also a watering pool in the middle of a generously sized courtyard. The stables, it has been

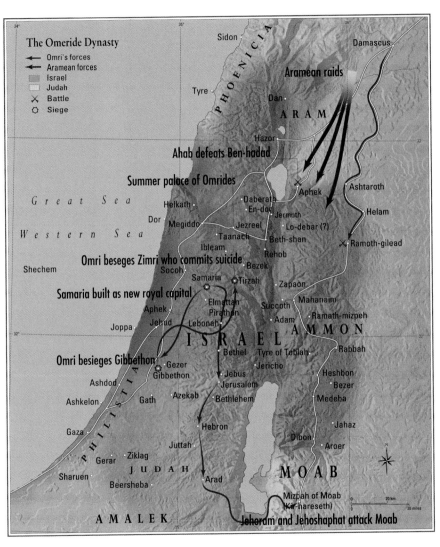

The Omeride Dynasty

← Omri's forces
← Aramean forces
▨ Israel
▧ Judah
✕ Battle
○ Siege

Sidon

Damascus

P H O E N I C I A

Tyre

Dan

Aramean raids

A R A M

Hazor

Ahab defeats Ben-hadad

Aphek ✕

Ashtaroth

Summer palace of Omrides

G r e a t   S e a

Helkath

Daberath
En-dor

Jermuth

Helam

Dor
Megiddo

Jezreel

Lo-debar (?)

W e s t e r n   S e a

Taanach

Beth-shan

Ramoth-gilead ✕

Ibleam

Rehob

Omri beseges Zimri who commits suicide

Bezek

Socoh

Shechem

Samaria ○Tirzah

Zapaon

Samaria built as new royal capital

Elmattan
Pirathon

Mahanaim

Succoth

Aphek

Ramath-mizpeh

Joppa

Jehud
Lebonah

Adam

A M M O N

I S R A E L

Bethel

Tyre of Tobiah

Rabbah

Omri besieges Gibbethon

Gezer
Gibbethon

Jericho

Heshbon

Ashdod

Jebus

Bezer

Ashkelon

Gath

Azekab

Jerusalem
Bethlehem

Medeba

Gaza

Hebron

Jahaz

P H I L I S T I A

Juttah

Dibon

Aroer

Ziklag

Gerar

J U D A H

Arad

M O A B

Sharuen

Beersheba

A M A L E K

Mizpah of Moab
(Kir-hareseth)

Jehoram and Jehoshaphat attack Moab

0   20 km
0   20 miles

*Above: Solomon's descendants were frequently
threatened by their neighbors, such as the Omeride
Dynasty after Omri's reign.*

reckoned by excavators, were capable of housing around 450 horses at any one time and there was also a structure next door for housing numerous battle chariots.

Not that it seems Solomon necessarily believed he would have to use force of arms during his reign. Although quarrels and rivalries had made war in Mesopotamia endemic in the past, Solomon took care to ensure, as far as possible, that his relations with other kings in the area around Israel remained peaceful and mutually lucrative. The surrounding powers were all strong and intimidating in their own right, and would have made formidable enemies. In

Below: Southern Judea, part of Solomon's core territory over which he continued to rule.

Above: During the time of Solomon, cordial relations existed between the neighboring lands – later monarchs were forced to pay tribute to the Assyrians, however.

this context, his display of war matériel was actually all part of his diplomatic initiative, designed to persuade other rulers that his prestige was commensurate with theirs. This is a game that has been played many times among the world's major powers since the days of King Solomon, and is still being played around the world today.

War was a regular feature in Mesopotamia, as its many different states and tribes fought each other for land and resources and sometimes for supremacy. Consequently, every state had its army, some of them better equipped and more effective than others, but the greatest military power of all was the Assyrian Empire. Assyria was, in fact,

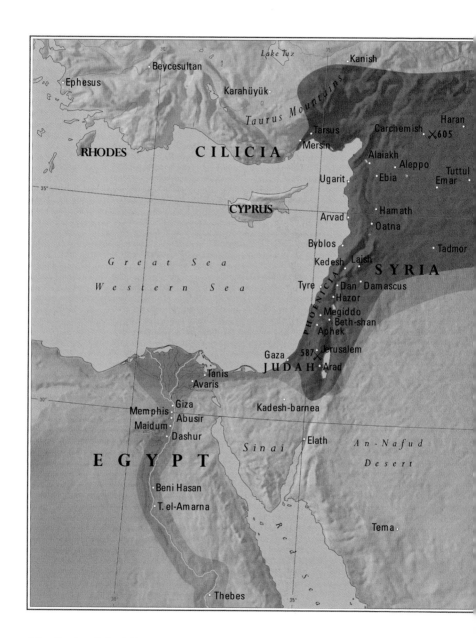

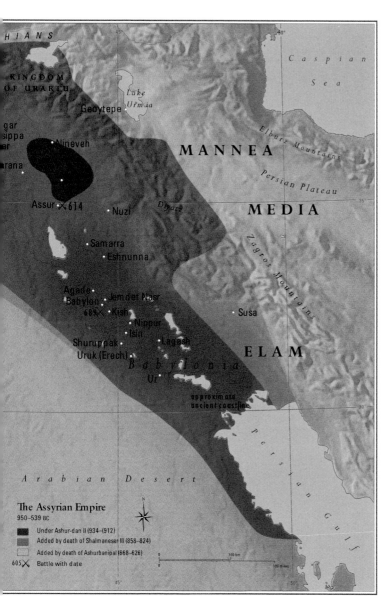

HIANS

KINGDOM
OF URARTU

gar
sippa
ar

rana

Geoytepe

Lake
Urmia

*Nineveh

Assur ╳614

*Nuzi

Diyala

*Samarra
*Eshnunna

Agade
Babylon*
689 ╳ *Kish
*Nippur
*Isin
Shuruppak* *Lagash
Uruk (Erech)*
*Ur

*approximate
ancient coastline*

Jemdet Nasr

B a b y l o n i a

C a s p i a n

S e a

Elburz Mountains

MANNEA

Persian Plateau

MEDIA

Zagros Mountains

*Susa

ELAM

P e r s i a n

G u l f

A r a b i a n   D e s e r t

The Assyrian Empire
950–539 BC

▨ Under Ashur-dan II (934–(912)
▨ Added by death of Shalmaneser III (858–824)
☐ Added by death of Ashurbanipal (668–626)
605 ╳ Battle with date

N

0   100 km
0   100 miles

*Left: The
Assyrian
Empire
expanded
toward
Palestine,
down the
coastal road
to Egypt
and along
the King's
Highway.*

Solomon's Kingdom   97

the world's first military state, much like Sparta, which was famously one of the city-states of Ancient Greece, a place where the preoccupation with war superseded all other activities.

In 1815, the British poet Lord Byron described Assyrian warfare in his poem "The Destruction of Sennacherib" (an eighth-century BC ruler of Assyria) as a wave of deadly destruction that spread terror and death in its path.

"The Assyrian came down like a wolf on the fold
And his cohorts were gleaming in purple and gold;
And the sheen of their spears was like stars on the sea
When the blue wave rolls nightly on deep Galilee."

This dread effect was first achieved by the Assyrian chariots, which comprised the core of their forces. The first chariots they used were two-horse affairs, which they utilized for reconnaissance and in battle as mobile firing platforms: these afforded opportunities for fast-moving hit-and-run tactics with the added advantage of a quick getaway.

Chariots were favored, of course, in the circumstances of the battlefield, where their high mobility was such a great advantage. For more static warfare, such as sieges, the Assyrians employed escalade – climbing the walls of a fortress by means of ladders – and battering rams. They also used the tactic of mining: collapsing the walls of a fortress or city by digging under the foundations.

Assyrian infantry was also very effective. The Assyrian style of infantry was composed of several elements: spearmen, who carried short spears that measured less than a man's height, archers, with their accompanying shield bearers, and slingshooters. The purpose of slingshot fire was to fool an enemy into lowering their shields to protect themselves against the hail of stones. This, of course, exposed enemy soldiers to fire from the archers, who were then able to shoot above the shield wall and so kill them in large numbers.

An additional purpose for the archers, who had a range of up to 650 meters, was to soften up an enemy for a charge by the chariots and cavalry. In Assyrian warfare, cavalry was employed in large numbers, sometimes consisting of units comprising 1,000 horsemen.

Although missile weapons, such as spears and arrows, were extensively used by the Assyrians, their preferred tactic was the mighty frontal charge by chariots and cavalry, leading to ferocious hand-to-hand fighting. This could be as costly for the Assyrians as it was for their enemies. One of the inscriptions on which Assyrian rulers recorded their triumphs described, in the most bloodthirsty terms, a phyrric victory achieved by Sennacherib against the Elamites:

"I rushed upon the enemy like the approach of a hurricane... I transfixed the troops of the enemy with javelins and arrows... Humban-udasha, the commander in chief of the King of Elam, together with his nobles... I cut their throats like sheep... My prancing steeds... plunged into their welling blood as into a river; the wheels of my battle chariot were bespattered with blood and filth. I filled the plain with the corpses of their warriors like grass..."

The Assyrians launched annual campaigns in a bid to expand the borders of their territory, which was slowly moving across Palestine by means of the King's Road and the coastal route to Egypt. In Solomon's time, this presented few problems, but for his descendents it was to spell disaster. By the time Omri took the throne of Israel, the two divided kingdoms were sufficiently weakened by religious unrest and intermittent warfare with Syria and Transjordan that many of the outer territories were lost and the interior came under dire threat from the might of Assyria.

Meanwhile, another of Solomon's neighbors, in Egypt, was disposed to make a more amicable treaty with the Judeans. Like the Ancient Egyptian Pharoah Psusennes II, Solomon's other important neighbor, Hiram, the King of Tyre, was entirely willing to do business with the rich, illustrious, and powerful King of Israel.

Hiram, whose territory included the Phoenician littoral lying between Lebanon and the sea, owned the famous Cedars of Lebanon, an evergreen coniferous tree that grew up to 40 meters tall, with a trunk up to 2.5 meters in diameter. In addition, among Hiram's subjects were the highly skilled artisans of Gabal, who were lent to Solomon by their king for carving wood, fashioning stone, and casting bronze during the construction of the Temple in Jerusalem.

The two kings concluded

Left: The Assyrian cavalry were their strength, here shown disposing of an Arab band of nomads.

a commercial treaty in which Solomon undertook to send Hiram an annual supply of 20,000 measures of wheat for his household and 20 measures of oil. Solomon also exchanged territory for trees. As the first Book of Kings (Chapter 9, Verse 11) put it:

"Now Hiram the king of Tyre had furnished Solomon with cedar trees and fir trees, and with gold, according to all his

Below: Assyrian engineers could bring down the walls of a captured city, demolishing them quickly and expertly to allow troops inside.

desire, that then king Solomon gave Hiram twenty cities in the land of Galilee."

Like the artisans of Gabal, the trees were also destined for the Temple. The tree trunks were floated down the coastline to Jaffa and from there taken inland to Jerusalem and the Temple site.

The treaty with King Hiram furnished Solomon with another great benefit. He became acquainted with the Phoenician techniques in shipbuilding and gained experience of the method Phoenician merchants used in trade. Solomon's territory included the once independent state of Edom, which gave him possession of the port of Eloth (modern Elath) at the head of the Gulf of Aqaba.

There, Solomon oversaw the building of ships for which he provided crews from his own servants. The vessels embarked Phoenician ship masters and set sail south to trade with Arabia. From Arabia, Solomon acquired stocks of gold which, like the Cedars of Lebanon, went to beautify the Temple in Jerusalem as well as to fill the king's coffers.

This was the start of extensive trade between Solomon's kingdom and Arabia, in which caravans loaded with goods were able to cross the desert in only two or three days, with sufficient water to complete the journey.

Eventually, Solomon came to monopolize the caravan trade between southern Arabia and Mesopotamia and between the Red Sea and Palmyra in Syria. Along this route, which, then as now, could be a

gruelling experience, Solomon had an oasis dug at Tadmor, 225 kilometers northeast of Damascus.

Solomon, who monopolized the trade routes to both the east and west of the Jordan River, acquired a huge amount of revenue from merchants who paid dues to travel through his territories. His father, King David, had destroyed the Philistine monopoly of iron and iron manufacture, which gave Solomon the chance to exploit the iron industry.

Besides gold and iron, Solomon also claimed copper deposits. Here again, Phoenician craftsmen were of great value to the king. They were experts in setting up and operating copper furnaces

Opposite: Solomon made a great show of the might and wealth of his kingdom, impressing and winning the allegiance of his neighbours.

and refineries, and had already done so in Spain and the Mediterranean island of Sardinia.

With this, Solomon added another dimension to his rapidly growing wealth, for copper refining and exporting was an extremely lucrative business. In fact, Solomon pioneered nationwide production in the mining industry of the Wadi Arabah, which today comprises the border between modern Jordan and Israel that runs from the Dead Sea to the Red Sea.

In time, copper became King Solomon's chief export, which was carried as raw ore by his fleet from the port of Ezion-geber and exchanged for valuable imports in Arabian and east African ports.

Ezion-geber was, in fact, constructed for King Solomon

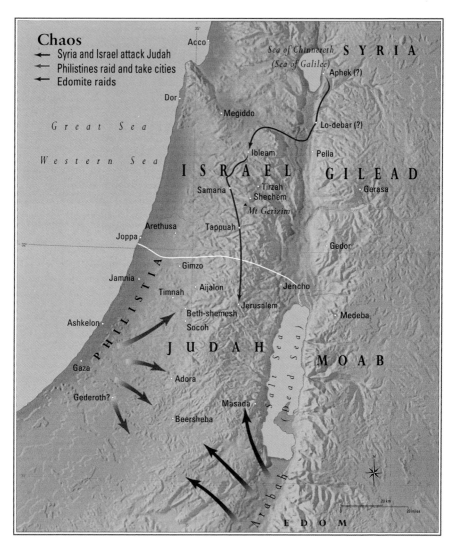

Chaos
← Syria and Israel attack Judah
← Philistines raid and take cities
← Edomite raids

Acco

Sea of Chinnereth
(Sea of Galilee)   S Y R I A

Aphek (?)

Dor

Megiddo

Lo-debar (?)

G r e a t   S e a

Ibleam   Pella

W e s t e r n   S e a   I S R A E L   G I L E A D

Samaria   Tirzah
            Shechem   Gerasa

▲ *Mt Gerizim*

Arethusa   Tappuah

Joppa

Gedor

Gimzo

Jamnia   Jericho

Timnah   Aijalon

Jerusalem

Beth-shemesh

Ashkelon   Socoh   Medeba

J U D A H   *Salt Sea (Dead Sea)*   M O A B

Gaza

Adora

Gederoth?

Masada

Beersheba

Arabah

E D O M

20 km
20 miles

*Above: During the reign of the Assyrian king
Tiglath-pileser, the king of Judah was forced to
appeal for help against enemies in all directions.*

by Phoenician sailors who afterward came to the port every three years or so. The first Book of Kings (Chapter 10, Verse 22) describes the arrangement:

"For the king had at sea a navy of Tharshish with the navy of Hiram: once in three years came the navy of Tharshish, bringing gold, and silver, ivory, and apes, and peacocks (a type of monkey)."

In the first verse of his poem "Cargoes" (1917), the British Poet Laureate John Masefield expanded on these imports, as carried by the large trading vessels of the time, such as the quinquireme, a ship with five banks of oars:

"Quinquireme of Nineveh from distant Ophir,
Rowing home to haven in sunny Palestine,
With a cargo of ivory,
And apes and peacocks,

Sandalwood, cedarwood, and sweet white wine."

The goods described were great luxuries. "Distant Ophir" has been variously identified as Great Zimbabwe, an important center for the gold trade, the African shore of the Red Sea, present-day Yemen, and even as far away as modern India. Needless to say, they added even more wealth to Solomon's already healthy treasury.

Just as productive was the trade in horses, which brought Solomon yet more revenues. Horses were essential in the ancient world, for travel or for war, so there was never any shortage of merchants anxious to trade in this living merchandise. Solomon acted as the middleman for the import of horses from Egypt and Kue in Cilicia in Asia Minor

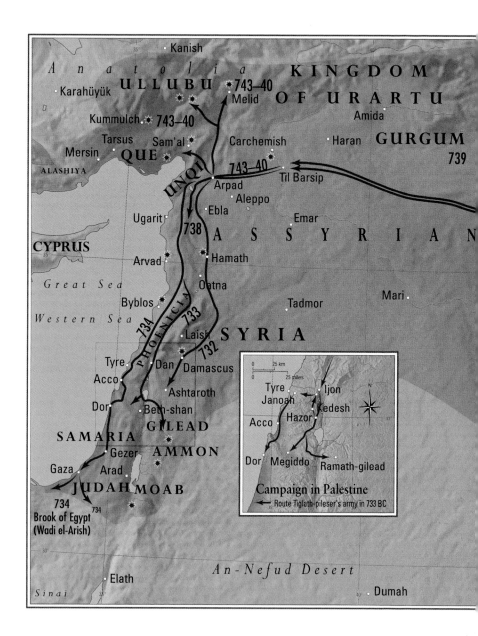

Kanish

A n a t o l i a

U L L U B U ★ 743–40 **K I N G D O M**

Karahüyük Melid **O F U R A R T U**

Kummulch ★ 743–40 Amida

Tarsus Sam'al Carchemish Haran **GURGUM**

Mersin **QUE** **739**

ALASHIYA UNQI 743–40 Til Barsip

Arpad

Aleppo

Ugarit Ebla

738 *A   S   S   Y   R   I   A   N*

CYPRUS Emar

Arvad Hamath

Great Sea Qatna

Byblos Tadmor Mari

Western Sea PHOENICIA 733 734

Laish **S Y R I A**

Tyre Dan 732

Acco Damascus

Ashtaroth

Dor Beth-shan

GILEAD

SAMARIA

Gezer **AMMON**

Gaza Arad

JUDAH MOAB

734

Brook of Egypt 734

(Wadi el-Arish)

An-Nefud Desert

Elath

Sinai Dumah

Campaign inset map:

0 25 km

0 25 miles

Tyre Ijon

Janoah Kedesh

Acco Hazor

Dor Megiddo Ramath-gilead

Campaign in Palestine

← Route Tiglath-pileser's army in 733 BC

Assyrian campaigns under Tiglath-pileser III

← Campaign with probable date
＊ Payment of tribute
□ Extent of the Assyrian empire

A S S Y R I A

M A N N E A

· Arbailu

M   P   I   R   E → 737

Persian

Plateau

Nuzi·

M E D I A

→ 744

Zagros Mountains

·Agade

·Babylon

·Susa

B a b y l o n i a

→ 731–29

Ur·

E L A M

Persian

Gulf

Left: The seasonal campaigns by the Assyrians changed in policy – conquered territory was incorporated into the empire rather than left as dependencies.

(Turkey). This was an area that had long been renowned for fine horses. When heavier chariots carrying four men were introduced into Mesopotamian warfare, each of them required the combined pull of four horses, and four horses per chariot was very lucrative business.

When it came to the business of government, Solomon opted for centralization, so that control devolved on him and his officers and ministers. He divided his realm into 12 administrative districts, each of which was obliged to send him a month's worth of taxes and labor. This was an innovation for Solomon's subjects, who had long been tribal.

Tribal squabbles were, by their very nature, a destabilizing factor. Centralization could not entirely get rid of this issue, but it went a long way toward calming the problem and reducing the chance that local interests would interfere with national imperatives.

The 12 new districts that Solomon had carved his empire into cut across old tribal boundaries. He imposed heavy taxation on these districts, to be paid to his treasury on a monthly basis, and demanded "bondservice" – the duty to provide free labor – from the non-Israelite Amorites, Hittites, Perizzites, Hivites, and Jebusites. He also enforced special levies for special tasks.

In this context, the first Book of Kings (Chapter 5, Verses 13-17) describes the arrangements made to provide

Opposite: Solomon welcomed many visitors, including the Queen of Sheba, from surrounding territories; all were impressed with his hospitality.

labor and services for building the Temple in Jerusalem.

"And king Solomon raised a levy out of all Israel; and the levy was thirty thousand men. And he sent them to Lebanon, ten thousand a month by courses: a month they were in Lebanon, and two months at home... And Solomon had threescore and ten thousand that bare burdens, and fourscore thousand hewers in the mountains; Beside the chief of Solomon's officers which were over the work, three thousand and three hundred, which ruled over the people that wrought in the work. And the king commanded, and they brought great stones, costly stones, and hewed stones, to lay the foundation of the house."

King Hiram of Tyre was by no means the only monarch who thought it worthwhile to do business with King Solomon. In fact, he became something of a royal celebrity whose fame spread through all the surrounding nations. He was a "must" on the visiting list of other monarchs who, it was said, came from far and wide to hear Solomon's wisdom

According to the Bible, Solomon's most famous visitor was the Queen of Sheba, who was much more a guest than the romantic interest of myth, legend, and Hollywood movies. The Queen is reputed to have traveled a distance of some 1,930 kilometers from her own realm by the Red Sea to Jerusalem to consult Solomon and benefit from his wisdom.

While she was about it, she also witnessed his luxurious lifestyle. As the first Book of Kings (Chapter 10, Verses 1-10) records:

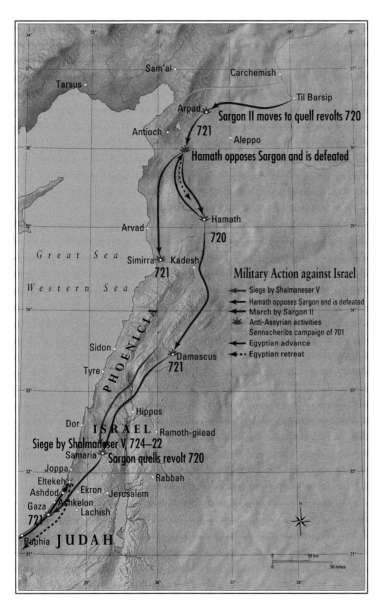

Map labels:

Tarsus
Sam'al
Carchemish
Til Barsip
Arpad
Sargon II moves to quell revolts 720
Antioch
721
Aleppo
Hamath opposes Sargon and is defeated
720
Arvad
Hamath
Great Sea
Simirra · Kadesh
721
Western Sea

Military Action against Israel
— Siege by Shalmaneser V
← Hamath opposes Sargon and is defeated
← March by Sargon II
⚔ Anti-Assyrian activities
Sennacheribs campaign of 701
← Egyptian advance
•••• Egyptian retreat

Sidon
Damascus
721
Tyre
PHOENICIA
Hippos
Dor · ISRAEL · Ramoth-gilead
Siege by Shalmaneser V 724–22
Samaria · **Sargon quells revolt 720**
Joppa
Eltekeh
Ashdod · Ekron
Gaza · Ashkelon · Jerusalem · Rabbah
721 · Lachish
Raphia **JUDAH**

0   50 km
0   50 miles
N

*Left:
The final
destruction of
Israel came
about in
721-720BC,
during a bout
of military
actions.*

Solomon's Kingdom 113

Above: Vines such as these, near Lachish, are the symbol of the prophets who warned of the invasion of Jerusalem by the Assyrians.

"And when the Queen of Sheba heard of the fame of Solomon concerning the name of the Lord, she came to prove him with hard questions... And she came to Jerusalem with a very great train, with camels that bare spices, and very much gold, and precious stones: and when she was come to Solomon, she communed with him of all that was in her heart. And Solomon told her all her questions: there was not any thing hid from the king, which he told her not. And... the Queen of Sheba (saw) all Solomon's wisdom, and the house that he had built, and the meat of his table, and the sitting of his servants, and the attendance of his ministers, and their apparel, and his cupbearers...

And she said to the king, 'It

was a true report that I heard in mine own land of thy acts and of thy wisdom.

Howbeit I believed not the words, until I came, and mine eyes had seen it: and, behold, the half was not told me: thy wisdom and prosperity exceedeth the fame which I heard.

Happy are thy men, happy are these thy servants, which stand continually before thee, and that hear thy wisdom. Blessed be the Lord thy God, which delighted in thee, to set thee on the throne of Israel: because the Lord loved Israel for ever, therefore made he thee king, to do judgment and justice.' And she gave the king an hundred and twenty talents of gold, and of spices very great store, and precious stones: there came no more such abundance of spices as these which the queen of Sheba gave to King Solomon."

The grandeur, wealth, and fame that so greatly impressed the Queen of Sheba among other monarchs of the day did, however, cause a problem for the only monotheistic state in a world of pagan religions and practices. The Jewish faith had always been fiercely protected simply because it was unique in the ancient world; but the basic flaw that affected its integrity was Solomon's fondness for women, in particular his many marriages to numerous foreign – and therefore pagan – wives and the "import" of concubines from the same source.

The diplomatic gains Solomon made by this marital policy were, of course, a vital part of his statecraft and brought immense material and political benefits to his kingdom. But as he aged,

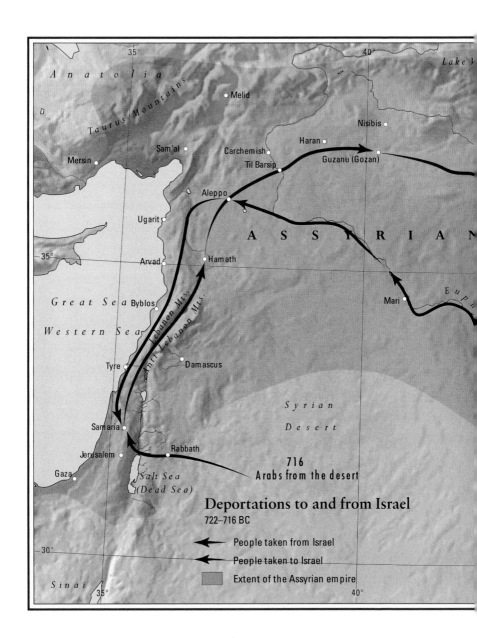

Deportations to and from Israel
722–716 BC

716
Arabs from the desert

← People taken from Israel
← People taken to Israel
▨ Extent of the Assyrian empire

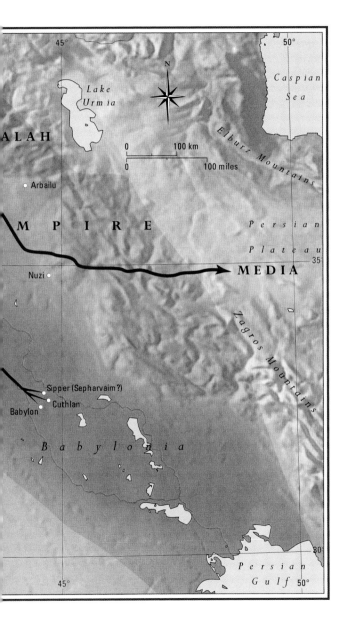

Left: Assyrian policy, once a nation had been conquered, was to deport the citizens of that land. In Israel's case, people were moved into the country, while others were sent to far provinces of the empire.

he was unable to keep his private life separate from his public identity. As a means of reassuring his wives and the kings and families to which they belonged, he had long permitted his wives and concubines to retain their own religions and to bring to Israel their own shrines, idols, and other religious paraphernalia. Idolatry is, of course, fiercely denounced in the Bible, all the more so after Solomon himself began to offer sacrifices and build shrines to the pagan gods he had allowed his women to bring into his kingdom.

This was roundly condemned in the first Book of Kings (Chapter 11), which reads:

"But King Solomon loved many strange (foreign) women... Of the nations concerning which the Lord said unto the children of Israel, Ye shall not go in to them, neither shall they come in unto you: for surely they will turn away your heart after their gods: Solomon clave unto these in love... For it came to pass, when Solomon was old, that his wives turned away his heart after other gods... For Solomon went after Ashtoreth the goddess of the Zidonians, and after Milcom the abomination of the Ammonites. And Solomon did evil in the sight of the Lord, and went not fully after the Lord, as did David his father. Then did Solomon build an high place for Chemosh, the abomination of Moab, in the hill that is before Jerusalem, and for Molech, the abomination of the children of Ammon. And likewise did he for all his strange (foreign) wives, which burnt incense and sacrificed unto their gods."

The Book of Kings threatened Solomon with

divine punishment amounting to the destruction of his kingdom, although this was apparently postponed for a time because of God's love for his father, King David.

However, from a purely political point of view, King Solomon was clearly heading for trouble toward the end of his long reign. Naturally, traditional, religious Jews in Israel were offended when their king played court to foreign, pagan gods, but beyond that, there were practical considerations. For a start, the taxes Solomon imposed on his subjects were excessive and burdensome.

The effective break up of

Below: Solomon, known for his wisdom, is shown here sitting in judgment in a painting by Nicolas Poussin.

the tribal system caused by the centralization of government may have lessened the danger of tribal quarrels, but it strained, or even severed, longstanding ties and loyalties. This was a social change that proved deeply disturbing to the more traditionally minded. In addition, the "bondservice" Solomon demanded for his building projects was resented because of the way it disturbed family, farming, and communal life.

People in the north of Israel had their own dissatisfaction with Solomon for his sale of 20 cities in Galilee to King Hiram of Tyre as part of the price of his aid in the building of the Temple. This, of course, separated them from their brethren in Israel and placed them under the rule of a foreign, non-Jewish king.

Solomon's subjects in the south, by contrast, made no such sacrifice, for Solomon had secured that border by marrying the pharoah's daughter. The feeling naturally grew in the north that the south was being unduly favored.

This was more than a mere jealousy, though. The northerners were infuriated, for as they complained to Rehoboam, Solomon's son, in the first Book of Kings Chapter 12, Verse 4):

"Thy father made our yoke grievous: now therefore make thou the grievous service of thy father, and his heavy yoke which he put upon us, lighter, and we will serve thee."

These words undoubtedly foreshadowed rebellion – and that rebellion already had a potential leader. Jeroboam,

Opposite: Jerusalem, Solomon's pride and joy, was a well-fortified city that could resist invaders well.

son of Nebat, of the tribe of Ephraim and one of Solomon's officials, had ambitions to become king of the ten tribes of northern Israel – the other two tribes lived in Judah, in the south – and he was greatly influenced by the prophet Ahijah of Shiloh, who had long been prophesying the division of Israel and Judah, which fitted in nicely with Jeroboam's plans.

After King Solomon died in 931BC, it seemed Jeroboam might have his chance. But any bids he might have made to divide the kingdom and

Rehoboam, who was at the time 41 years old, was not a particularly pleasant or diplomatic character, although a lot of his arrogance actually hid a certain weakness. His subjects suspected that he was going to be too much like his father, which raised the prospect of more royal demands on the people's money, time, and patience.

Even so, Rehoboam had one chance to prove them wrong. When his subjects insisted that his coronation take place at Schechem, in the north of what was still, at that juncture, a united kingdom, he agreed, only to be confronted with vociferous demands that he reduce taxes.

He asked for, and was

establish his rule in the north were quickly upset.

Rehoboam, the son of Solomon and the pharaoh's daughter Naamah, was proclaimed king and his early conduct made Jeroboam hopeful that his own plans could succeed.

given, three days to come up with an answer. He took counsel, but received two completely opposing opinions. His older councillors, who had formerly served King Solomon, advised him that his best course of action was to lower taxes in order to gain popular favor. His younger councillors, who were more aggressive, told him that he ought to raise taxes so as to emphasize his authority.

Unfortunately, Rehoboam sided with the younger councillors, who had probably echoed his own opinion on the matter. He gave his subjects his decision and rubbed in it with the rather callous message: "My father chastised you with whips, but I will chastise you with scorpions."

At this, the ten tribes of northern Israel immediately declared independence, repudiated their loyalty to the royal House of David, and seceded from Rehoboam's kingdom. They asked Jeraboam to become their king. He accepted, chose the town of Shechem as his capital, and set about rebuilding and fortifying it.

To emphasize the division between the two halves of the now divided kingdom, Jeroboam set up two shrines, or "golden calves" at Dan and Bethel, which marked the northern and southern borders of his new realm. He told his subjects that the "golden calves" represented God. The people of the new, separate, Kingdom of Israel, Jeroboam instructed, were not to travel any more to Jerusalem for the purposes of worship and prayer. Instead, they must bring their sacrifices to the two shrines he had erected.

Above: The Assyrians were one of the dominant military forces in the area. The Assyrian infantry is shown in this bas-relief from the palace of Ashurbanipal at Nineveh attacking the Elamites, who were mostly archers.

These shrines became known as "the way" or "the sins" of Jeroboam. Subsequently, Jeroboam's "sins" led to a return to idolatry. Ahab, who became King of Israel in 869BC, 40 years after Jeroboam's death, sanctioned the worship of Ba'al, a fertility god whose cult was widespread in ancient Phoenicia and Canaan. His wife, the famous wicked woman of the Bible, Jezebel, was a particularly devoted adherent.

Jeroboam's shrines, echoing the episode during the exodus from Egypt when the children of Israel built a golden calf and worshipped it, were doubtless the cause of a warning he is said to have received, prophesying that his kingdom would come to a catastrophic end.

In the first Book of Kings (Chapter 13, Verses 3-5) Jeroboam was offering incense at Bethel when a prophet from the Kingdom of Judah appeared, saying:

"This is the sign which the Lord hath spoken; Behold, the altar shall be rent, and the ashes that are upon it shall be poured out. And it came to pass, when king Jeroboam heard the saying of the man of God, which had cried against the altar in Bethel, that he put forth his hand from the altar, saying, Lay hold on him.

And his hand, which he put forth against him, dried up, so that he could not pull it in again to him. The altar also was rent, and the ashes poured out from the altar, according to the sign which the man of God had given by the word of the Lord."

Jeroboam's hand was cured, after he pleaded with the

prophet for its restoration but, although he continued to reign for 22 years and died of natural causes in 910BC, the dire prediction eventually came true.

In 717BC, the kingdom of Israel was attacked by the Assyrians under King Shalmaneser V. The Assyrians laid siege to Samaria, which by then was the capital of the kingdom of Israel.

Shalmaneser died before the siege was concluded, to be succeeded by Sargon II, who saw the city finally fall after three years. Sargon recorded the end of Samaria in terse terms:

"Samaria I looked at, I captured; 27,280 men who dwelt in it I carried away."

Although numerous refugees managed to get away and reach safety in Judah, where they increased its population five times over, a majority of the ten tribes living in Israel were captured and taken into exile in Assyria.

When Israel divided from Judah in 930BC, the formerly vast kingdom of Solomon shrank appreciably. The non-Israelite states – Moab and Edom – regained their independence. In Judah, however, King Rehoboam seems to have lost his sense of reality. Somehow, he failed to recognize the secession of the northern tribes and sent a tax collector – possibly Adoniram, who had performed the same function for Solomon – to gather in the dues he reckoned were owed to him.

Needless to say, Adoniram was not made welcome in Israel. He was, in fact, stoned. Rehoboam, who was nearby, having followed his tax collector to see how he got on, took to his heels and fled back to Jerusalem.

Once back in Jerusalem, Rehoboam organized an army of around 180,000 men, intending to suppress what he considered to be a rebellion. But the prophet Shemaiah proclaimed that it was the will of God that the once united monarchy should be divided.

At that, Rehoboam abandoned his plans. There never was a formal war between Israel and Judah during Rehoboam's 17-year reign, but there were skirmishes from time to time. Rehoboam's army also skirmished with Damascus and Edom, but with little real damage on either side.

Nevertheless, Rehoboam took the precaution of building a defensive network of 15 fortified cities, including the mightiest of them at Lachish. This, though, did not protect Judah from a really serious crisis that occurred in the fifth year of Rehoboam's reign. In 926BC, the Ancient Egyptian Pharaoh Shoshenq, also known as Shishak, invaded Judah, together with his Ethiopian allies.

Together, they sacked Jerusalem and went on a binge of looting all over the Kingdom of Judah. The Temple in Jerusalem did not escape the carnage and the decorative gold shields made for King Solomon were among the booty that was taken. Afterward, Rehoboam replaced them with bronze shields, which were, in themselves, an earnest of the misfortune the Temple had suffered.

Shoshenq, returning home in triumph, commemorated his offensive at Karnak, where a

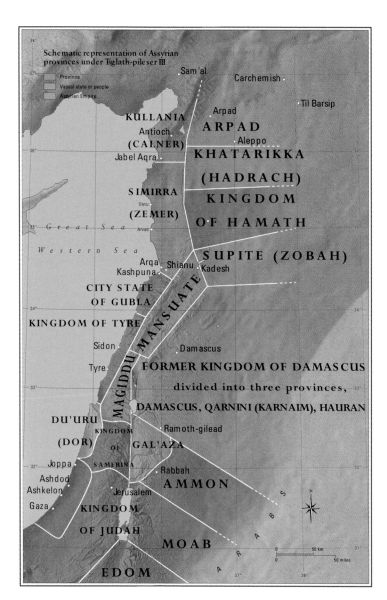

Schematic representation of Assyrian
provinces under Tiglath-pileser III

- Province
- Vassal state or people
- Assyrian Empire

Sam'al

Carchemish

Til Barsip

KULLANIA

Antioch

(CALNER)

Arpad

ARPAD

Aleppo

Jabel Aqra

KHATARIKKA

(HADRACH)

SIMIRRA

Usnu

(ZEMER)

KINGDOM

OF HAMATH

Great Sea

Arvad

Western Sea

SUPITE (ZOBAH)

Arqa

Shianu

Kashpuna

Kadesh

CITY STATE

OF GUBLA

KINGDOM OF TYRE

MANSUATE

MAGIDDU

Sidon

Damascus

Tyre

FORMER KINGDOM OF DAMASCUS

divided into three provinces,

DAMASCUS, QARNINI (KARNAIM), HAURAN

DU'URU

Ramoth-gilead

KINGDOM

(DOR)

of **GAL'AZA**

Joppa

SAMERINA

Ashdod

Rabbah

Ashkelon

AMMON

Jerusalem

Gaza

KINGDOM

OF JUDAH

MOAB

EDOM

*Left: The
Assyrians
eventually
overran
what had
once been
Solomon's
consolidated
territories.*

Above: Solomon was believed to have been *responsible for writing the Book of Proverbs, part of which is illustrated here: "Pride goeth before destruction, and an haughty spirit before a fall."*

series of sculptures in a wall of the one of the temples depicted the Pharaoh holding in his hand a number of prisoners, among other figures, and the names of the Judean towns he had captured inscribed in stone. These towns were those that had been fortified by Rehoboam.

After this humiliation, Rehoboam refortified his kingdom so that most of the approaches to Jerusalem through the Judean mountains were guarded by large, powerful fortresses. Even so, there were gaps in the defenses. The mountainside that led up from the Judean desert in the east had no defensive works, nor did the border with the Kingdom of Israel because, incredibly perhaps, King Rehoboam did not recognize it as an independent state.

But whatever Rehoboam believed, the prestigious kingdom he had inherited from Solomon was shattered within a year of his father's death. In subsequent centuries, it was to crumble even further, until little was left intact to show that Solomon's Israel had ever existed.

Just over a century after the destruction of the northern Kingdom of Israel, in 612BC, the once mighty Assyrian Empire that had vanquished it fell in its turn. Subsequently, many descendants of the exiles were free to scatter throughout the Middle East.

Some 75 years after that, when Jews from the Kingdom of Judah were themselves taken into captivity by the Babylonians, many of these descendants joined them. But the ten tribes of Israel as such were never restored, nor indeed were they found, despite several efforts made by medieval Christian explorers to locate them.

The Kingdom of Judah was never the same again after the Babylonian exile and, although the valiant Hasmoneans were to know 103 years of independence in the 2nd and 1st centuries BC, this was only achieved under the aegis of Rome. After the Romans installed their nominee King Herod in 37BC, the Jews were not to know independence again for almost 2,000 years.

The Rise and Fall of Babylon

The empire of Babylon, which was the superpower of Mesopotamia some 2,500 years ago, was the focus of the most dazzling Golden Age of ancient times. Babylonian architecture, art, astronomy and mathematics, canals and irrigation systems, and its legal code, introduced by its sixth ruler, Hammurabi, placed Babylon head and shoulders above its rivals.

Babylon started out as one of several small kingdoms in Mesopotamia, rivaling each other for supremacy over the fertile land between the rivers Tigris and Euphrates. But Babylon became splendidly equipped to prevail in this context when an exceptional ruler, Hammurabi, an Amorite, became its king in around 1795BC. At that stage, power in Mesopotamia resided in four other states: Eshunna, which controlled the upper Tigris river, Larsa which was established in the river delta, the kingdom of Elam to the east, and Assyria to the north. Hammurabi's first moves reflected this power play situation. During his first 30 years as king, he built up the defenses of Babylon by raising the height of the city walls. At the same time, he expanded the city's temples, which served the creator god, Enki, and the god of the atmosphere, Enlil.

After that, though, Hammurabi was drawn into the network of rivalries in 1766BC when the kingdom of Elam invaded the Mesopotamian plain, destroyed Eshunna, and seized several small cities. But the undoing of Elam came about when Babylon and Larsa discovered that the Elamites were attempting to set the two of them against each other and start a war. Instead,

Hammurabi and the king of Larsa joined forces to crush the Elamites, although Larsa proved somewhat laggard and Babylon had to do the greater part of the work.

At that, the war between Babylon and Larsa transpired after all, with the former gaining a brilliant victory that gave Hammurabi control over the lower Mesopotamian plain.

This was the start of an expansion that saw the

Below: The dragon was the sacred animal of the Babylonian god Marduk.

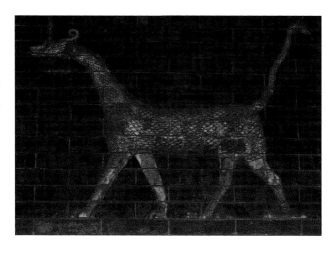

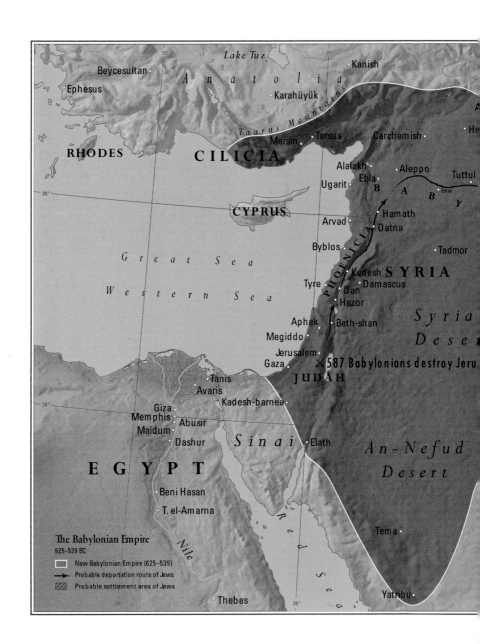

Lake Tuz

Beycesultan

Ephesus

A n a t o l i a

Kanish

Karahüyük

Taurus Mountains

RHODES

CILICIA

Mersin

Tarsus

Carchemish

He

Alalakh

Aleppo

Tuttul

Ebla

Ugarit

B

A

B

Y

Emar

CYPRUS

Hamath

Arvad

Qatna

Byblos

Tadmor

G r e a t   S e a

Kedesh

SYRIA

Tyre

Damascus

PHOENICIA

Dan

W e s t e r n   S e a

Hazor

S y r i a

D e s e r

Aphek

Beth-shan

Megiddo

Jerusalem

× 587 Babylonians destroy Jeru

Gaza

JUDAH

Tanis

Avaris

Kadesh-barnea

Giza

Memphis

Abusir

Maidum

Dashur

S i n a i

Elath

A n - N e f u d

D e s e r t

EGYPT

Beni Hasan

T. el-Amarna

Tema

The Babylonian Empire

625–539 BC

New Babylonian Empire (625–539)

Probable deportation route of Jews

Probable settlement area of Jews

Nile

Red Sea

Yatribu

Thebes

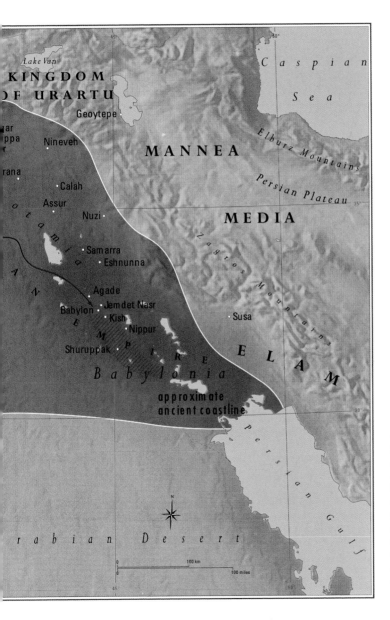

Left: After crushing the Assyrians, Babylon turned its attention to the "fertile crescent", eventually creating a huge empire across the region.

Babylonian armies dispose of Eshuna and all the other major city-states in the region except for Aleppo and Qatna. With

Below: The city of Babylon, seen from the north, as it is believed to have looked at the time of Hammurabi's rule.

that, Babylon assumed central control over all Mesopotamia and Hammurabi was able to turn to more peaceful, more intellectual pursuits. The greatest of these endeavours was his Code of Law, which set

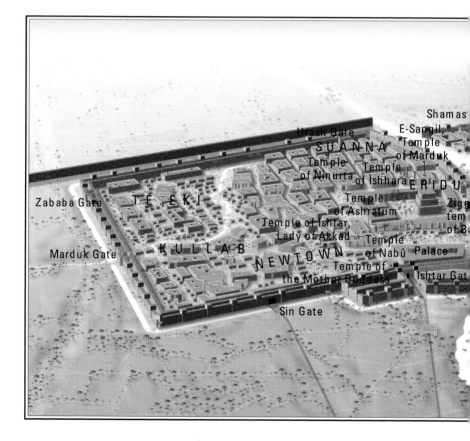

Shamas
E-Sangil,
Urash Gate
Temple
SUANNA
of Marduk
Temple
Temple
of Ninurta
of Ishhara
ERIDU
Temple
Zabba Gate
TE.E.KI
Zigg
of Ashratum
tem
Temple of Ishtar,
of B
Lady of Akkad
Temple
Marduk Gate
KULLAB
of Nabû
Palace
NEWTOWN
Temple of
the Mother Goddess
Ishtar Gat

Sin Gate

a standard of civilized behavior that still influences legal practices today.

Hammurabi himself believed that he had been chosen by the gods to bring the law to his subjects. He stated: "Anu (Enki) and Bel (Enlil) called by name to me, Hammurabi, the exalted prince, who feared God, to bring about the rule of righteousness in the land."

The laws of Hammurabi can still be seen, inscribed on a basalt slab or stele some 2.2 meters tall that was discovered in Iran in 1901 by the French Egyptologist Gustave Jéquier.

But, as often happens when great men take the helm, Hammurabi's successors could not match his standards, nor protect Babylonia from outsiders. Consequently, for over a 1,000 years after Hammurabi's death in around 1750BC, a series of invaders seized power in Babylon: the Hittites, the Kassites, the Assyrians, the Elamites, and the Assyrians again.

The Assyrian empire itself collapsed after the Chaldean leader Nabopolassar and

his son Nebuchadnezzar II conquered and plundered its capital, Nineveh, in 612BC and assumed control of Babylon. With that, Babylon at last acquired rulers that enabled it to rise above the perpetual rivalries that blighted Mesopotamia and retrieve the glory the city had enjoyed under Hammurabi.

Babylon had been destroyed in an uprising against its Assyrian masters in 648BC, so Nabopolassar and his son enjoyed a clean slate on which to start again. They did not merely rebuild the ruined city, but created an entirely new metropolis with splendid buildings. One was the rectangular stepped ziggurat surmounted by a temple dedicated to the creator god, Marduk, which was probably the model for the Tower of Babel. Another was the famous "hanging gardens", a triumph of ingenious engineering and artistic imagination that was to become one of the Seven Wonders of the ancient world.

More prosaically, Nebuchadnezzar ringed the whole city with a strong defensive wall made of brick.

The eight gates that led into the city of Babylon were dedicated to the eight gods of Chaldea, the most famous among them being the beautiful blue-tiled Ishtar gate, built for the goddess of fertility. A magnificent royal palace was constructed on the banks of the river Euphrates, together with multi-story housing that was well in advance of its time and paved streets.

Under Nebuchadnezzar II,

Opposite: The Ishtar Gate, one of the eight gates that led into the ancient city of Babylon, has been restored and now resides in the Pergamon Museum in Berlin, Germany.

Opposite: The first four chapters of the Book of Daniel, as illustrated here in the twelfth-century Lambeth Bible, feature the Babylonian ruler Nebuchadnezzar and his dealings with Daniel.

who succeeded as king after the death of his father in around 604BC, Babylon became the trade center of Mesopotamia, handling goods from Arabia and as far away as India. Babylon was also an intellectual centre, excelling in literature, science, mathematics, astrology, and astronomy, which afterward became the basis for modern astronomy.

Nebuchadnezzar also had an important function in Babylonian religion. Alhough not thought to be divine himself, he was regarded as the mediator between the gods and the people. One of his duties was to perform rituals for the worship of Marduk, Ishtar, and Shamush, god of the Sun and of justice.

But unlike his long-ago predecessor Hammurabi, Nebudchadnezzar did not enjoy the luxury of an extended period of peace. Much of his 43-year reign was occupied with war as he confronted Babylon's powerful rival, Egypt, for control of the area of land that is now the Middle East. Their rivalry was never resolved, but the fluctuating fortunes of Babylon in this context gave states that had once been under Assyrian rule hope of regaining their independence.

One of these states was Judea. The fall of the Assyrian empire had given Judea and other Mesopotamian states freedom from a brutal occupation. Assyria was the world's first military state, equipped with all the latest weaponry and chariot-power. As might be expected, the Assyrians governed their conquests in repressive martial style.

But any sense of relief that the Judeans might have felt at the removal of a cruel master did not last for long. There were other contenders waiting in the wings to take over where Assyria had left off, and Judea was sited on the natural battleground between Egypt (to the south) and Babylon (to the east). Unfortunately for Judea, it was inevitable that Babylon should be the next in line to dominate the area.

Nevertheless, hopes for independence did not fade in the face of this reality, and the Judeans were greatly encouraged in 601BC when Nebuchadnezzar's army, impressive though it was, came to grief in an attempted invasion of Egypt.

The events of this time are featured in the Bible, and Nebuchadnezzar's defeat was actually forecast in the book of the Jewish prophet Jeremiah (Chapter 46, Verses 3-12) in a highly dramatic passage that also gave indications of the weaponry employed by the Babylonian army and its allies:

"Order ye the buckler and shield, and draw near to battle. Harness the horses; and get up, ye horsemen, and stand forth with your helmets; furbish the spears, and put on the brigandines (coats of mail).... Let not the swift flee away, nor the mighty man escape; they shall stumble, and fall toward the north by the river Euphrates... Egypt riseth up like a flood, and his waters are moved like the rivers; and he saith, I will go up, and will cover the earth; I will destroy the city and the inhabitants thereof. Come up, ye horses; and rage, ye chariots; and let the mighty men come forth; the Ethiopians and the Libyans,

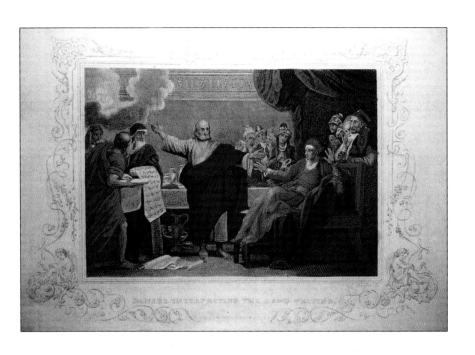

that handle the shield; and the Lydians, that handle and bend the bow. For this is the day of the Lord God of hosts, a day of vengeance, that he may avenge him of his adversaries: and the sword shall devour, and it shall be satiate and made drunk with their blood... The nations have heard of thy shame, and thy cry hath filled

Above: The doom of Nebuchadnezzar's heir, Belshazzar, was also prophesied, this time at a feast, when Daniel translated mysterious writing that appeared on the wall as meaning the days of his kingdom were numbered. The king was killed the very same night.

the land: for the mighty man hath stumbled against the mighty, and they are fallen both together."

The idea that the Babylonians and Egyptians

would dispose of one another, to the benefit of Judea, was not exactly correct. Nor was the notion that the Judeans could stand against Babylon as and when they rebelled against Nebuchadnezzar. The Babylonian king, after all, could field a professional army numbering up to 50,000 men, backed up by militias and a phalanx of chariots that were more powerful and destructive than they had ever been.

Babylonian chariots were much heavier than previously and carried up to four men: the driver, an archer, a shield bearer, and a man with a short spear. Their combined weight required the pulling power of four horses.

Chariot strategy had changed since earlier days, when they had been used to circle enemy forces: instead, the drivers took them directly into the opponents' battle formations, causing immense damage and death.

Against this panoply of armed might, the Judeans, led by their king, Jehoiachin, probably had no more than about 10,000 men, and of course they lacked the immense wealth and resources that were available to the Babylonians. Their only option, when they finally rebelled in 597BC, was for the Judeans to shelter behind the walls of Jerusalem, which, inevitably, Nebuchadnezzar placed under siege.

The siege was brief, for King Jehoiachin soon surrendered and paid a huge tribute, which included gold and silver from the Temple's treasury. Jehoiachin was further punished with exile, together with 10,000 of Judea's leading citizens and a number of craftsmen.

This, of course, removed the elite, who might lead another rebellion, and the artisans with the skills to supply the weaponry the rebellion might need. Also, with Jehoiachin gone, Nebuchadnezzar was able to put his own puppet, Zedekiah (whom he expected to be somewhat more pliable and obedient), on the Judean throne.

There was little hope of that. Zedekiah had his own ambition for freedom and, in this, he was encouraged by the wily Pharaoh Psammetichus II of Egypt. As the pharaoh doubtless hoped, Zedekiah began to formulate his own plans for a revolt only four years after his predecessor's surrender and drew into his plot other states in Syria which were similarly burdened by Babylonian rule: Edom, Ammon, and Moab, together with Tyre and Sidon in Phoenicia.

Thus bolstered by his allies, King Zedekiah went ahead and declared Judean independence in 591 BC. Nebuchadnezzar tried to intimidate Zedekiah into surrendering, but he refused to emulate his predecessor King Jehoiachin. At that, Nebuchadnezzar marched on Jerusalem at the head of a mighty army that included a siege train and cavalry; its strength, once again, comprised up to 50,000 men.

Despite the superior strength of his army, Nebuchadnezzar was mindful of the perils that might lurk in the Jordan Valley and the Judean mountains, where Israelite guerrillas had once destroyed other armies unwise enough to enter them. Instead, he took the long way around to reach Jerusalem, along the coastal plain. On the way, several cities surrendered to the Babylonian army without a fight. Kedesh, Megiddo, and Aphek attempted resistance, only to be swiftly crushed by escalade, a tactic that employed ladders to scale fortified walls and was much speedier than laying a city under siege.

The overwhelming power of Nebuchadnezzar's army was such that he was able to attack more than one city at a time. In 588BC, by which time he had finished what were, in effect, mopping up operations, Nebuchadnezzar was ready to assault Jerusalem.

Inside the city was a population of around 20,000 people, plus another 20,000 refugees who had fled there from the path of the advancing Babylonian army. King Zedekiah, meanwhile, was relying on a promise of military aid from another Egyptian pharaoh, Apries, but he also had more solid advantages. A century earlier, King Hezekiah had built up the walls of Jerusalem, providing them with towers, and constructed a second wall inside the first. This second wall was a massive affair, 6 meters wide and made of large boulders. In addition, Hezekiah had provided Jerusalem with an internal water supply, linked to the Gihon Spring, which could not be interfered with from outside.

Nebuchadnezzar's siege of Jerusalem began on October 10, 587BC, only to be broken off when Pharaoh Apries kept his promise and advanced into Judea from Egypt. Potentially, this move could have trapped the Babylonians between the Egyptian army and the walls of Jerusalem. But that possibility soon vanished when Nebuchadnezzar intercepted the Egyptians north of

Gaza and thrashed them. Nebuchadnezzar was soon back outside Jerusalem and the siege resumed.

Jeremiah, the prophet of doom, was inside the city at this time, in prison for daring to suggest that Jerusalem was going to fall. As an eyewitness, his description of the siege was truly grim. He told how the Babylonians constructed long, shallowly inclined siege ramps made of wood and rock, which allowed them to roll their siege engines – specifically their battering ram – up to the higher reaches of the walls. The ram was an entire tree trunk strapped with iron or bronze and equipped with a sharp iron head that could unpick the stones in a wall as it rammed them.

Below: The ruins of Jerusalem confirm its deliberate destruction by the Babylonians.

Above: Isiah is regarded as the greatest of the Old Testament prophets. His prophecies were concerned with political and spiritual matters regarding Babylon, and foretold the empire's eventual destruction.

The ram was suspended from ropes so that it could be repeatedly swung against the weakest point in a wall. The defenders could, in theory, prevent the operation of the ram by various means: they might kill or injure the crew, set fire to the ram, or cut the ropes that held it.

Just how effective these methods could be depended on the ability of the attackers to fight off the Judeans seeking to destroy the ram. It would seem, though, that the Judeans had some success, for this time, Jerusalem did not fall quickly or easily.

The siege lasted for 18 months, until famine and disease swept through the city. There are horror stories in the Biblical Book of Lamentations (Chapter 4, Verse 10) that record how starving mothers killed their own children, then cooked and ate them. The ram kept battering away at the wall until at last, on July 9, 586BC, the northern wall of Jerusalem was breached.

Some of the defenders managed to get away from the street fighting that followed and shelter in the heavily fortified complex of the Temple of Solomon. There, they held out until August 4, but on August 7, Nebuchadnezzar decided to finish the fight once and for all and ordered the destruction of the temple.

Once the Babylonian forces were inside Jerusalem, King Zedekiah and his entourage attempted to escape and head for the Judean mountains. They got as far as the river Jordan before a Babylonian patrol caught up with them. Zedekiah was taken to the

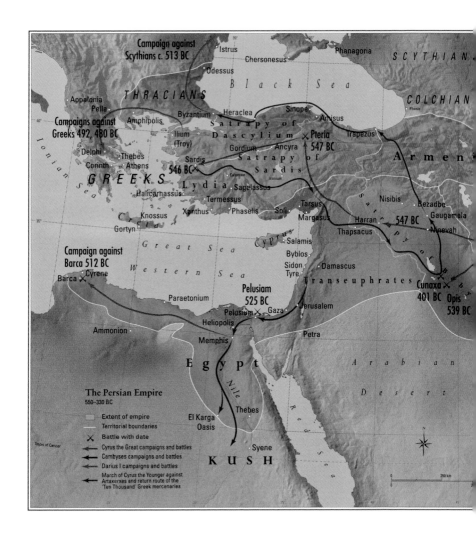

Campaign against Scythians c. 513 BC

Istrus
Chersonesus
Phanagoria
Odessus
Black Sea
SCYTHIAN
COLCHIAN
Appalonia
Pella
THRACIANS
Phasis

Campaigns against Greeks 492, 480 BC

Amphipolis
Byzantium
Heraclea
Sinope
Amisus
Ilium (Troy)
Satrapy of Dascylium
Pteria ×
547 BC
Trapezus
Ionian Sea
Delphi
Thebes
Gordium
Ancyra
Armen
Corinth
Athens
Sardis
Satrapy of Sardis
546 BC ×
GREEKS
Lydia
Sagalassus
Iconium
Calpenae
Halicarnassus
Termessus
Tarsus
Nisibis
Bezadbe
Knossus
Xanthus
Phaselis
Soli
Margasus
Harran
547 BC
Gaugamela
Gortyn
Creta
Thapsacus
Ninevah
Cyprus
Salamis
Great Sea
Byblos

Campaign against Barca 512 BC

Western Sea
Sidon
Tyre
Damascus
Transeuphrates
Cunaxa ×
401 BC Opis
539 BC
Barca ×
Cyrene
Pelusiam 525 BC
Paraetonium
Pelusium × Gaza
Jerusalem
Heliopolis
Ammonion
Petra
Memphis
Egypt
Arabian
Desert
Nile
The Persian Empire
550–330 BC
El Karga Oasis
Thebes
Red Sea
Syene
Ammonion

- Extent of empire
- Territorial boundaries
- × Battle with date
- ← Cyrus the Great campaigns and battles
- ← Cambyses campaigns and battles
- ← Darius I campaigns and battles
- ← March of Cyrus the Younger against Artaxerxes and return route of the 'Ten Thousand' Greek mercenaries

KUSH

250 km

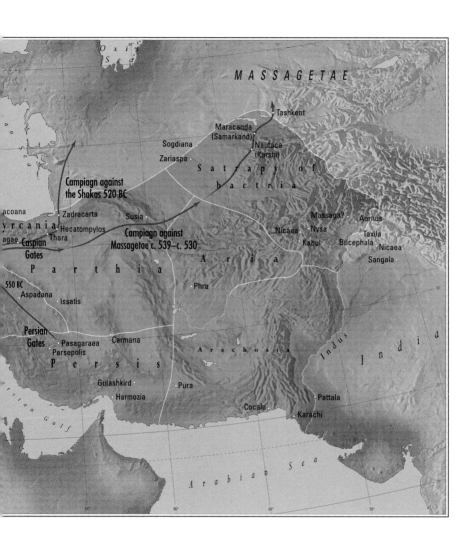

Above: During the rule of Cyrus, in around 550BC, the Persian Empire began to extend its frontiers westward through Asia Minor and Mesopotamia. Persia was to replace Babylon as the dominant superpower.

northern town of Riblah, where Nebuchadnezzar had established a base. There, the king was punished in gruesome fashion. His sons were killed as he watched and this ghastly scene was the last thing he saw, for afterward his eyes were put out and he was loaded down with chains and sent to Babylon a captive.

Zedekiah was not the only one. A number of Jews were taken to Babylon to spend a prolonged captivity in the Babylonian capital. Most of them, it seems, were members of the aristocracy and their families, together with other prominent individuals capable of causing more trouble had they remained in Jerusalem. Soldiers and skilled craftsmen who could be of use to the Babylonians were also taken, but farmers, who were less likely to prove troublesome, stayed behind, still in possession of their land.

Nebuchadnezzar died in 562BC, 25 years after the conquest of Jerusalem, but his successors as kings in Babylon were neither as effective nor as successful as he had been.

The Babylonian Empire began to decline, something that had been predicted by the prophet Isaiah throughout the first 39 chapters of the Book of Isaiah, in which he spoke of the eventual fall of Assyria and Babylon and the coming of a kingdom of peace and the Messiah, bringing with it freedom from exile for the Jews and the restoration of Zion.

When the next powerful empire-builder, Cyrus II the Great, became king of Persia in around 550BC, Persia began to expand westward through Mesopotamia and Asia

Above: The prophet Ezekiel preached to the Jews during their captivity in Babylon, his emphasis on repentance and the judgment of God.

Minor, quickly filling the place Babylon had once occupied as the dominant Mesopotamian superpower. For the captive Jews, there was an unexpected bonus from this change in power. In 516BC, Cyrus allowed the Jews to return to Judea after 70 years in their Babylonian captivity. Some 40,000 Jews, the descendants of the original exiles, returned to Judea, a land most of them had never seen before.

Alexander the Great

King Alexander III of Macedon was one of the greatest, if not the greatest, military leaders of ancient times. He conquered the whole of the world as it was known in the 4th century BC and is said to have wept on learning that there was no more territory to acquire. Alexander was a military prodigy, demonstrating at a remarkably young age a hallmark of genius: simply "knowing" the right tactics to employ to win battles and executing them with dash and flair.

The Greek city-states of Athens and Thebes, which had been forced to pledge allegiance to Alexander's father, saw the succession as a chance to gain independence from the inexperienced young monarch. But Alexander was already a powerful warrior-leader and needed Greek support for his forthcoming war against King Darius of Persia. He had to move quickly because Darius was trying to bribe the Greeks to come over to his side with gifts of gold. The Thebans were

Opposite: Alexander became King of Macedon in 336BC at just 20 years of age, after his father, King Philip, was assassinated.

willing to join Darius, but were frightened off when Alexander's army appeared at the city gates and demanded their surrender. They gave in at once. Other Greeks were more willing to

back Alexander, and gathered at the Isthmus of Corinth, where they elected the young king Captain-General of the Hellenes (Greeks) against Persia. His father had held the title before him. Only Sparta, the military city-state, refused to join.

Alexander moved to secure his northern borders at the River Danube against the Thracians and Illyrians. He moved first against the Thracians and deceived them about the power of his forces by sending out archers and slingers against them. This lulled the Thracians into believing Alexander's army was weak and ineffective. Assured of an easy victory, the Thracians attacked a force they thought could do no more than throw rocks and arrows at them. Instead, they encountered Alexander's crack troops, his infantry. The Thracians surrendered, but

Opposite: Corinth was a city-state in antiquity, situated on the Isthmus of Corinth, where Alexander gathered his Greek allies.

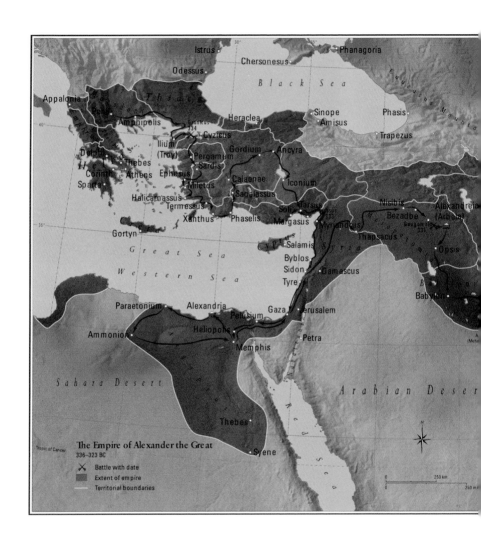

Above: Alexander's empire stretched across almost the entire known world at the time, taking Greek culture and civilization far beyond the boundaries of his home until he reached the Indus River and his troops rebelled; he died on the journey home.

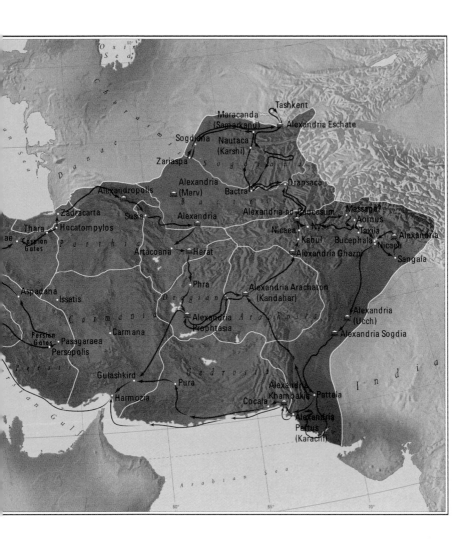

the Illyrians were a tougher proposition. They managed to isolate Alexander and his small force from the rest of his army, so Alexander put on a special military show. He ordered his troops to parade in front of them, marching in close, disciplined formation while carrying their spears. As they went, Alexander's forces carried out intricate military maneuvers. The Illyrians were so fascinated by this strange performance that they were taken by surprise when Alexander suddenly ordered his cavalry to charge against them. Alexander's infantry joined in, setting up a cacophony of noise by striking their swords on their shields and yelling the Macedonian war cry. The Illyrians ran back to their fortress as Alexander ordered his catapults into action. The Illyrians were soon defeated.

Alexander crossed the Hellespont in 334BC and landed in Turkey. His force was so large that it took 100 triremes (three-tiered oar ships) to transport it. When Darius III of Persia learned of Alexander's arrival, he refused to take the young king seriously. It was a grave mistake, which Darius would bitterly regret. But Alexander also miscalculated, thinking Darius was weak and ineffective. As it happened, it was true that the Persian style of warfare did not employ the sort of cunning Alexander liked to employ. Alexander believed, therefore, that it would be easy to outwit the Persian king. He did not have to bother. Darius was so convinced Alexander could do nothing against him that, even as the Macedonian monarch marched through Turkey, he mounted no serious challenge. Nor did Darius dispute the liberation of Greek towns, which surrendered one by one. Nothing, it seemed, would stop Alexander, and he was deep in Persian territory when, at last, Darius realized he must act. The Persian and Macedonian armies met at Granicus River, near the site of Troy, in May 334BC.

The locale of this battle, on the banks of the river, was very much to the disadvantage of the Persian forces. Their forte was deploying huge forces on the battlefield and seeking victory through sheer weight of numbers. This might have been effective on broad, flat plains, but riverbanks were cramped, muddy, and slippery and afforded little or no room for large forces or chariots. At Granicus, the Persians arrayed their infantry behind the cavalry on the east bank. Alexander placed his heavy phalanxes (massed infantry in rectangular formation) in the center, with cavalry on either side. Alexander took the Persians by surprise by attacking as soon as his troops were in place. The Macedonian cavalry and light infantry made the first attack, from the left, with Alexander and his personal bodyguards charging through on horseback to smash into the Persian center. Many Persian nobles were killed, although one, Spithridates, managed to hit Alexander on the head with his axe. Spithridates was preparing to finish him off when he was killed by one of Alexander's officers, Cleitus the Black.

A gap had now opened up in the Persian line and Alexander's cavalry surged through to fall upon the Persian infantry in the rear. The infantry fled and Darius' cavalry retreated. The stunning victory was not lost on the Greek cities, who saw an opportunity to relieve themselves of the taxes imposed by the Persians. In return, Alexander asked only that they join the League of the Isthmus of Corinth, which meant the money would instead come to him. Meanwhile, the Persian navy made threatening gestures in the hope of provoking Alexander. With no navy of his own, he refused to be riled.

Eventually, the Persians gave up and left for the naval base at Halicarnassus. Meanwhile, Memnon of Rhodes, Commander of the Greek mercenaries in service with Darius, and his son-in-law Orontobates had installed themselves in the city. Memnon was determined to resist Alexander and deployed catapults to prevent his entry. The catapults were so effective that Alexander was forced back.

Memnon, encouraged, sent in troops, but Alexander's infantry managed to break through the walls. In the ensuing fight, Orontobates was killed. It was only a matter of time before Halicarnassus fell to Alexander, so Memnon sought to spoil the party by setting it on fire. Unfortunately, a wind sprang up, spreading the fire and destroying vast areas of the city.

The defeat at Granicus River taught King Darius a sober lesson: from now on he would take personal charge of his army. Darius' first task was to gather a force, and he combed his empire to recruit as many men as he could find. Darius chose the Pinarus River in southern Anatolia as the next stage. There was, though, one lesson Darius had failed to learn: a riverbank favored Alexander's smaller, but more mobile, army. In November

Above: Alexander sent his army to Persepolis along the Royal Road, looting and destroying it.

333BC, the king drew up his forces in a deep formation along the narrow coastal plain, with their backs to the hills. This was a big mistake, for the Persians were wrongly placed.

Darius discovered his error when Alexander led his cavalry against the Persian left flank and cut gaps in their formation. The Persians were routed. Meanwhile, his cavalry broke the Persian right flank. Alexander personally led his cavalry in a direct attack on the king's chariot. Darius' horses had been injured and were threatening to throw him. He jumped out instead, threw away his royal diadem, leapt onto a horse, and galloped off. His troops lost heart and were quick to surrender or, like their king, run away.

In 332BC, Alexander resolved to seize Tyre, the only Persian port not to surrender to him. Tyre, which stood partly on the Mediterranean coast, partly on an offshore island, was of paramount importance. It was the main base of the Persian navy and presented a major threat to Alexander's forces. Alexander still had no navy of his own, so he resorted to diplomacy. It proved impossible. The Tyreans declared they were neutral. When he tried a second time, he lost patience, killed their envoys, and threw their corpses over the city wall. Alexander's engineers fell back on one of his earlier plans: to build a causeway one kilometer long that would stretch as far as the island. Alexander also ordered the building of two towers, each 46 meters high, at the end, where he positioned siege machines. The Tyreans sent fireships – old transports filled with wood, pitch, sulfur, and other flammable materials – out to strike the causeway. The fire burned the towers and siege machines. Alexander had to think of another way.

Alexander realized he must create a navy. The only way, it seemed, was to obtain vessels from captured towns along the coast. Then the Persian navy returned to find the cities along the coast under Alexander's control. This meant their ships were also under his control.

News of his victories inspired the Cypriots to send another 120 ships; Alexander now led a navy of 200 ships and, with this force, sailed to Tyre and began blockading the port. Always innovative, Alexander had battering rams fitted to the slower vessels and used them to find a weak spot in the walls. The breach served as a platform for a heavy bombardment, with all Alexander's ships taking part. The army stood by, waiting for the moment they could force their way into Tyre. The 40,000 citizens of Tyre were at their conqueror's mercy. It was said he was so enraged at the loss of his men that, as punishment, he destroyed half the city. He pardoned the king, but took revenge on 30,000 citizens and foreigners, who were sold into slavery.

The destruction of Tyre was a grim warning to other towns in the area, and most quickly surrendered, except, that is, for Gaza, which stood on a hill and was heavily fortified. Gaza had a great deal to lose, for it was a center of lucrative trade. Alexander mounted three assaults on Gaza before his army managed to take it. After the surrender, the entire male population was executed and the women and children were sold as slaves.

Alexander proceeded to Egypt, where the Persians were hated. He received a heartfelt welcome and was greeted as the new pharaoh. He proceeded to Syria and crossed the Euphrates and Tigris, heading for the heart of the Persian empire. This far, Alexander met no opposition, but the Persian king, Darius III, had been preparing revenge. Once again, Darius built up a massive army, expecting to defeat Alexander by weight of numbers. They met on the battlefield at Gaugamela, which lay on the Persian plain. In the Persian royal tradition, Darius took up a position at the center of his forces, alongside his best infantrymen. Alexander, meanwhile, divided his men in two and prepared to lead

the left wing. His most trusted
general, Parmenion, led the
right. The Macedonian infantry
formed a phalanx and headed
for the center of the Persian
line. King Darius ordered his
chariots into action, but they
ran into the Agrianians, 1,000
ferocious Macedonian mountain
men. To Darius' horror, the
Agrianians made short work of
his chariots. Alexander led a
charge at the weakened Persian
center. When Darius' charioteer
was killed, the rumor spread
that the king had died. At this,
the Persian battle line fell apart
and Darius was once again
forced to run.

Alexander set off in pursuit,
but was temporarily diverted
by the fabled wealth of Persian
cities like Babylon and Susa.
Alexander headed for these
cities, and in Susa found more
riches than he had ever seen:
six times the yearly income of

the city-state of Athens. While
Alexander enriched himself,
Darius was eaten up with fury.

Bent on revenge, the Persian king was heading east, hoping to raise another army. There

Above: Alexander's arrival was greeted with great pleasure by some of his conquests, including Egypt and, as shown in this painting by Johan Georg Platzer, the city of Babylon.

was little chance of that. The satraps (provincial governors), although nominally loyal to Darius, realized, as he did not, that it was futile to resist Alexander and capitulated to him instead. The ambitious satrap of Bactria, Bessus, had his own ideas of how to deal with Darius. He stabbed him, leaving him mortally wounded but alive when Alexander's scouts came across him. The king held the hand of one of the Macedonians, thanking him for not leaving him to die deserted and alone. Darius, the last king of the Achaemenid dynasty of Persia, was given a full-scale military funeral.

Bessus had notions of succeeding Darius, but so did Alexander, who regarded Bessus as a brutal usurper and had him hunted down and killed. Then he headed for Susa, which he captured before

moving against Pasargadae, in the province of Persis.

Persis was not such a simple conquest. Alexander would have to make his way through a narrow mountain pass called the Persian Gates: the pass was tailor-made for ambush, and Ariobarzanes, the satrap of Persis, had set exactly this type of trap. For once, Alexander made a serious miscalculation: he thought he would not have to face any more enemies along his march through Persia. But as soon as he entered the Persian Gates, Ariobarzanes' men pelted the Macedonians with rocks while his archers shot a blizzard of arrows at them and catapults hurled boulders. Alexander's forces suffered heavy casualties, but the young king had sufficient forces left to surround Ariobarzanes and break through his defenses.

This was the last stand of

the Persian forces. After Persis, Alexander went to Persepolis, which he captured and looted four months later. Alexander had by now conceived a plan to conquer the rest of the world, which, in his time, was thought to end in eastern India. In 327BC, he began his next campaign, against the kings of India. He started by attacking the Sogdian Rock, a fortress north of Bactria in the Himalayan region. Presenting himself before the fortress, Alexander ordered the garrison to capitulate, which they refused to do. Alexander called for volunteers to climb the cliffs that underpinned the fortress. Around 300 of Alexander's men were experienced mountaineers and climbed the cliff in the dark, using tent pegs and lines made of flax. Thirty lost their footing, fell, and were killed, but the remainder made it to the top and, to signal their success to the Macedonians waiting below, waved to them with pieces of linen. Alexander sent a herald to shout out the news that the advance posts of the Sogdian Rock were about to be assaulted. The news came as a shock to the defenders. They were so shocked, in fact, that they surrendered.

The site of Alexander's last siege was the present-day city of Swat in Pakistan. In Alexander's time, it was called Pir-sar, or Aornos by the Greeks, and was a vital target because it threatened Macedonian supply lines. Aornos was a particularly tough objective, for it was set on a spur in the mountains above narrow gorges of the upper Indus River. The fortress was vulnerable on its north side but the way was obstructed by a deep ravine. Alexander needed his catapults close enough for their missiles to reach inside, so he set his men to building a mound of earth as a bridge across the ravine. By this means, the Macedonians managed to get within reach of a low hill close to Aornos. But the defenders had been alerted and rolled boulders down the hill into their path. Alexander's men were unable to move forward and the defenders celebrated for three days by loudly beating drums. Then, inexplicably, they retreated. Alexander, realizing he had won, used a rope to haul himself to the summit of the hill. Once there, he set up altars to Athena, the Greek goddess of victory, in thanks.

Alexander's next enemy was King Porus, whose realm was located near present-day Bhera. The two kings met in battle at Kshatriya, on the River Hydaspes. Porus arrayed his forces on the south bank of the nearby River Jhelum, which was sufficiently deep and fast-running to prevent Alexander's forces from making a successful crossing. Alexander, however, found a more friendly crossing upstream and led a small force over. A dismayed Porus sent cavalry and chariots to confront him, but he sent them packing and killed their leader, Porus' son. Porus sent in the bulk of his army, which comprised cavalry on both left and right flanks, with elephants at the front and infantry behind. Alexander answered by dispatching his mounted archers to shower the left wing with a mass of arrows. Once they were in disarray, he launched his own cavalry and destroyed them. Porus ordered his elephants to charge, but they

Opposite: Rembrandt's depiction of Alexander demonstrates his legendary reputation as an unparalleled military force.

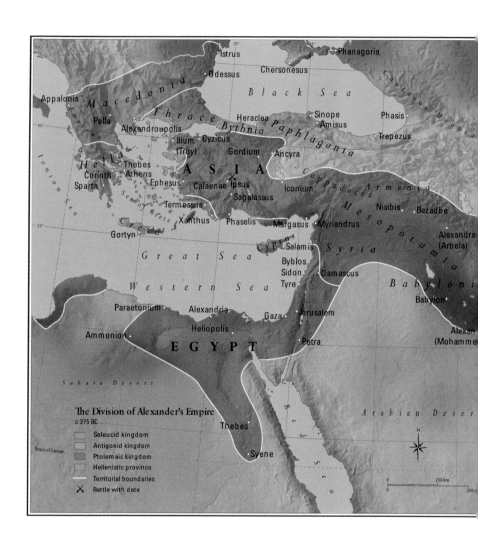

The following place names and labels appear on the map:

Istrus
Phanagoria
Odessus
Chersonesus
Appalonia
Black Sea
Macedonia
Epirus
Thrace
Heraclea
Sinope
Phasis
Caucasus Mountains
Pella
Amisus
Bythnia
Paphlagonia
Alexandroupolis
Trapezus
Ilium (Troy)
Cyzicus
Gordium
Ancyra
Hellas
ASIA
Thebes
Corinth
Athens
Ephesus
Calaenae Ipsus
Cappadocia
Armenia
Sparta
Sagalassus
Iconium
Mesopotamia
Termessus
Nisibis
Bezabde
Xanthus
Phaselis
Margasus
Myriandrus
Crete
Gortyn
Cyprus
Salamis
Syria
Alexandre (Arbela)
Great Sea
Babylonia
Byblos
Sidon
Damascus
Western Sea
Tyre
Babylon
Paraetonium
Alexandria
Gaza
Jerusalem
Alexan (Mohamm
Ammonion
Heliopolis
Petra
E G Y P T
Sahara Desert
Arabian Desert

The Division of Alexander's Empire
c. 275 BC

☐ Seleucid kingdom
☐ Antigonid kingdom
☐ Ptolemaic kingdom
☐ Hellenistic province
— Territorial boundaries
✕ Battle with date

Tropic of Cancer

Thebes
Svene
Red Sea

0   250 km
0   250

Above: After Alexander's untimely death, aged 32, his vast empire was divided among his generals, who fought jealously over the spoils. The matter was finally settled 20 years later, at the Battle of Ipsus, when the lands were doled out.

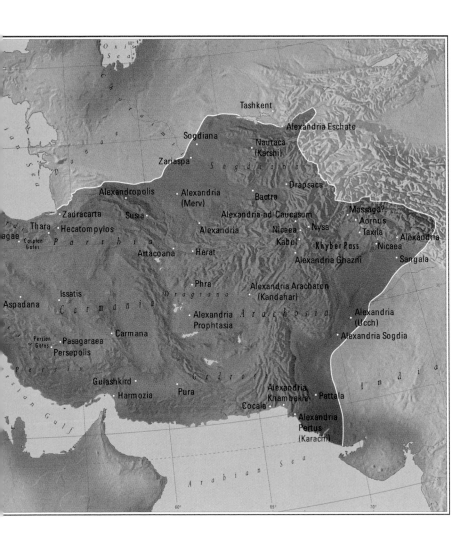

Tashkent

Alexandria Eschate

Sogdiana

Nautaca
(Karshi)

Zariaspa

S o g d i a n a

Drapsaca

Alexandropolis

Alexandria
(Merv)

Bactra

Alexandria-ad-Caucasum

Massaga?

Aornus

Zadracarta

Susia

Nicaea

Nysa

Taxila

Alexandria

Thara

Hecatompylos

Alexandria

P a r t h i a

Kabul

Nicaea

agae

Caspian
Gates

Artacoana

Herat

Khyber Pass

Alexandria Ghazni

Sangala

Phra

D r a g i a n a

Alexandria Arachaton
(Kandahar)

Issatis

C a r m a n i a

Alexandria
Prophtasia

A r a c h o s i a

Alexandria
(Ucch)

Aspadana

Carmana

Alexandria Sogdia

Persian
Gates

Pasagaraea

Persepolis

G e d r o s

I n d i a

P e r s i s

Gulashkird

Pura

Alexandria
Khambekia

Pattala

Harmozia

Cocala

Alexandria
Pertus
(Karachi)

Persian
Gulf

A r a b i a n S e a

60°

65°

70°

were surrounded and Porus' men were obliged to surrender.

This was Alexander's last battle. For where the kings of India had been no more successful in halting him than Darius, India itself brought his run to a close after eight years of campaigning and 17,700 kilometers of marching. He wanted to continue eastwards, but his troops had had enough, and when his priests said the gods had turned against him, he was forced to turn back.

Monsoons turned the land to swamp. The rains corroded their armor and rotted the supplies of grain. The rivers contained turbulent currents.

The way was punctuated by occasional battles against tribes along the Indus River, sandstorms, heat-stroke, flash floods, and poisonous snakes that entered the tents at night. The experience was so brutal

that almost two-thirds of them died. The survivors reached Macedon in December 325BC. Alexander returned to Babylon, where he considered himself King. He died on the afternoon of June 11, 323BC, aged only 32, possibly from malaria.

He died so suddenly that proper arrangements were not made for the future of his empire. The rivalry over the spoils was not settled for more than 20 years, until the Battle of Ipsus in western Anatolia in 301BC. After that, Alexander's empire was divided between his former generals. Cassander received Macedon; Lysimachus, Thrace; Seleucus, Mesopotamia, and Persia; and Ptolemy I Soter, the Levant (Middle East), and Egypt. Ptolemy founded a new dynasty in Egypt in 305BC. Alexander's conquests in India went to Chandragupta Maurya, the first Mauryan emperor.

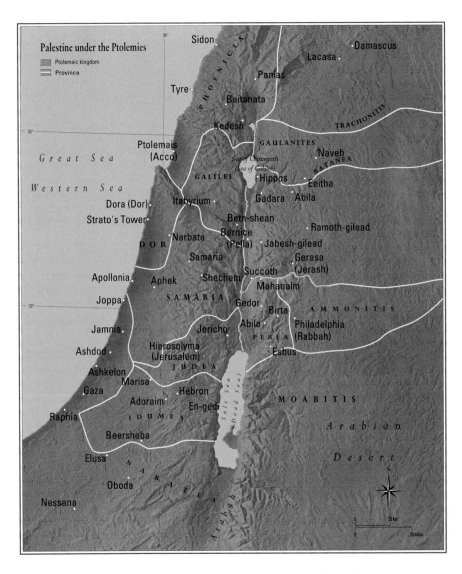

Palestine under the Ptolemies

- Ptolemaic kingdom
- Province

Sidon
Lacasa
Damascus
Panias
Tyre
Baitanata
PHOENICIA
TRACHONITIS
Kedesh
GAULANITES
Ptolemais (Acco)
Naveh
Sea of Chinnereth (Sea of Galilee)
BATANEA
Great Sea
GALILEE
Hippos
Eeitha
Western Sea
Dora (Dor)
Itabyrium
Gadara
Abila
Strato's Tower
Beth-shean
Ramoth-gilead
Narbata
Bernice (Pella)
Jabesh-gilead
DOR
Samaria
Gerasa (Jerash)
Apollonia
Aphek
Shechem
Succoth
Mahanaim
Joppa
SAMARIA
Gedor
AMMONITIS
Jamnia
Jericho
Abila
Birta
Philadelphia (Rabbah)
Ashdod
Hierosolyma (Jerusalem)
PEREA
Esbus
Ashkelon
JUDEA
Gaza
Marisa
Hebron
Salt Sea (Dead Sea)
MOABITIS
Raphia
Adoraim
En-gedi
IDUMEA
Arabian
Beersheba
Elusa
NABATEA
Desert
Oboda
Arabah
Nessana

0   20 km
0   20 miles

Above: General Ptolemy took control of Egypt after Alexander's death, founding a new dynasty.

The Revolt of the Macabbees

When Alexander the Great's conquests were divided, Judea went to Ptolemy and the dynasty of pharaohs he founded. From there, it passed to the Greek Seleucid empire, founded by Seleuceus, another of Alexander's generals. The Seleucids set about Hellenizing Judea, introducing Greek cultural influence that was not only pagan but hedonistic. This proved alluring to many Jews, but deeply insulted the more traditional and devout. Among these dissidents was the Jewish priest Mattathias and his sons.

The crunch in Judea came after 175BC, when the Seleucid king, Antiochus IV Epiphanes, started to issue a series of decrees banning Jewish religious practices in Judea. At this, the High Priest Mattathias ben Theophilus made a protest that sparked off a full-scale rebellion. He refused to make sacrifices to the Greek gods, then killed a Jewish man who offered to do so in his place. The Hellenization to which they and their growing number of

Above: The Maccabees resented the influence of Hellenistic Greek culture, which they perceived as hedonistic and pagan.

supporters objected represented the antithesis of orthodox Judaism. Pagan practices were bad enough, but it went further than that. Hellenized Jews deserted traditional Judaism and embraced the religious and cultural practices of the Greeks.

Jewish males were by tradition circumcized at the age of eight days to indicate their covenant with God, but Hellenized ones resorted to artificial measures to disguise the physical signs of the operation. They ate Greek food, abandoning the laws of kashrut.

One of these laws forbade pork, so it was an insult when the elderly Mattathias was

The Revolt of the Macabbees 177

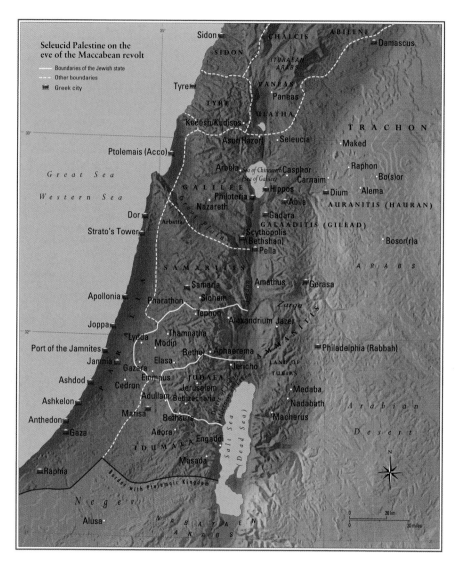

**Seleucid Palestine on the
eve of the Maccabean revolt**

—— Boundaries of the Jewish state
--- Other boundaries
▥ Greek city

Sidon

CHALCIS

ABILENE

Damascus

SIDON

ITURAEAN
ARABS

Tyre

PANEAS

Paneas

TYRE

ULATHA

Kedesh/Kudisos

Asor(Hazor)

Seleucia

TRACHON

Maked

Ptolemais (Acco)

Great   Sea

Arbela   *Sea of Chinnereth*   Casphor
(Sea of Galilee)   Carnaim

Raphon

Bo(s)or

Western   Sea

GALILEE   Hippos

Dium   Alema

Philoteria

Abila

AURANITIS (HAURAN)

Nazareth

Dor

Arbatta

Gadara

GALAADITIS (GILEAD)

Strato's Tower

Scythopolis
(Bethshan)

Bosor(r)a

Pella

SAMARIA   Amathus   Gerasa

A R A B S

Samaria

Apollonia

Pharathon

Sichem

Zarqa

Tephon

Joppa   Alexandrium Jazer

Thamnatha

Lydda   Modin

Aphaerema

Philadelphia (Rabbah)

Port of the Jamnites

Bethel

Jamnia   Elasa

Jericho

LAND   OF
TUBIAS

Gazara

Ashdod   Cedron   Emmaus   JUDAEA

Jerusalem

Medaba

Ashkelon   Adullam   Bethzecharia

Nadabath

Arabian

Anthedon   Marisa   Bethsura

Macherus

Gaza   Adora

Desert

Engaddi

IDUMAEA

N

Raphia   *Border with Ptolemaic Kingdom*

Masada

*Salt Sea
(Dead Sea)*

N e g e v

Alusa   NABATAEAN
ARABS

0   20 km
0   20 miles

*Above: Tensions between the Jews and their
Hellenistic rulers sparked a rebellion led by Judas.*

ordered to slaughter a pig as a sacrifice and eat its flesh. Mattathias responded by killing the Seleucid officer who had come to deliver the order.

After that, the elderly priest, his sons, and supporters fled to Gophna, in the Judean hills, where they organized a guerrilla army to confront the forces King Antiochus was bound to send against them. Secure for a while in the mountains, the rebels trained in guerrilla warfare such as surprise and hit-and-run attacks, ambushes, or night-time assaults, which were the only tactics open to them given their comparatively small numbers and lack of armaments. They carried primitive farm implements and home-made weapons such as slings and maces.

It soon became evident that King Antiochus IV Epiphanes did not understand the power of guerrilla fighting nor the zeal of the rebels to uphold their laws and traditions. Nor, it seems, did the king imagine the military skills of Judas, Mattathias' third son, who succeeded as leader of the revolt after the death of his father in 166BC. Judas later acquired the surname "Macabbeus", meaning hammer or sledgehammer. Believing he was facing a minor uprising of no military merit, Antiochus sent a small army, led by some of his lesser generals, to deal with Judas and his forces.

Judas realized they were very unlikely to defeat the Seleucid army in a direct confrontation and embarked on battle only under favorable conditions, in valleys, where the battleground was naturally confined and it was difficult for the broad Seleucid phalanxes to deploy. There was also the psychological pressure of operating in what was, in effect, hostile country, for the presence of guerrillas lurking unseen in the mountain passes was unnerving.

All the same, the nuisance potential of guerrillas did not hinder all the effectiveness of large professional forces. Even a small Seleucid army had its advantages. They were strictly trained, well organized, and experienced. The Seleucids fielded both light and heavy infantry armed with javelins, spears, bows and slings, swift and deadly chariots, and elephant units. Among their "artillery" were battering rams and ballistas that hurled stones large enough to kill at a distance and propelled strongly enough to reach inside besieged cities.

The first encounter took place in a defile at Nahal El-Haramiah, a few miles east of Gophna, in 166BC. This steep-sided narrow gorge was the perfect setting for an ambush when Apollonius, the Seleucid military governor of Syria, was ordered to engage the rebels with a force of 2,000 soldiers. Judas had only 600 men. Nevertheless, he divided his tiny force into four groups and assigned two of them to block off each end of the gorge after the Seleucids, marching in two long lines of 1,000 each, had entered the defile. The third and fourth rebel groups were stationed on the slopes of the valley, ready to fall on the Seleucids once they were sealed in. Judas's plan worked perfectly and the gorge, crammed full of trapped Seleucid soldiers, became a scene of slaughter. Apollonius was killed early on, and his force was wiped out.

This shock defeat jolted Antiochus out of his

complacency. He doubled the army he assigned to another of his generals, Seron, who realized the mistake his predecessor had made. He avoided becoming trapped in mountain country by marching into battle along the Mediterranean coast. In addition, Seron made sure that there were greater distances between the columns of his army, to prevent the guerillas ensnaring all of them at once. Even so, Judas decided to deal with Seron and his forces in the same way as before. He divided his guerillas into groups and prepared another ambush. This time, it would take place in a narrow gorge at Beth-horon.

Seron was only a day's march from Jerusalem when Judas ordered his men into action. He virtually duplicated the method he had used at Nahal El-Haramiah and produced the same result. Seron was killed and so were 800 of his soldiers. Those who managed to survive were chased onto the surrounding plain as they fled.

Antiochus went incandescent with rage at this second failure. Next time, he resolved, he would take overall command of his army, and he appointed a regent, Lysias, to govern in his place. Antiochus chose three generals – Ptolemy, Nicanor, and Giorgias – to head a huge army numbering between 20,000 and 40,000 men with 7,000 cavalry. The Macabbeans, by contrast, had a mere 6,000 guerrillas. The three generals went to war in 165BC, but took care to avoid what had already been identified as "ambush country" in the mountains: they reached their base at Emmaus, near the Valley of Ajalon.

In the meantime, northeast of Jerusalem, Judas gathered

his own forces at Mizpah, northeast of Jerusalem, and moved to within reach of the Seleucid camp. He arranged his forces in squads, the largest numbering 1,000 men and the smallest only 10. These were intended to operate within the four divisions, each 1,500 strong, to be commanded by himself and his three brothers, Jonathan, Simon, and Johanan. The spies Judas had sent ahead told him the Seleucid general Giorgias was planning to copy Macabbean methods and mount an attack at night. Giorgas assumed the Macabbeans would not expect to be attacked under cover of darkness, since the Seleucids were themselves

Below: The hill country was an important tool in Judas's arsenal, providing him cover from which to attack the Seleucid ranks.

unaccustomed to it.

Georgias, confident of victory, moved into the hills with his 5,000 infantry and 1,000 cavalry. Judas, meanwhile, had learned of Georgias' battle plan and left with his entire army, except for a small rearguard of 200 men. The Macabbean camp fires were left burning, giving Georgias the impression that Judas' forces were still there. Georgias fell for it and attacked the empty camp while Judas' rearguard withdrew up the valley within sight of the Seleucid army. Giorgias immediately assumed that what he was seeing was the entire force attempting to get away. He set off in pursuit, only to be repeatedly attacked by small concentrations of rebels.

Judas, meanwhile, headed for the Seleucid camp with 3,000 of his men, only to find 18,000 of Georgias' soldiers, with cavalry, ensconced there, ready for a fight. Judas saw that the Seleucid phalanx was moving south while his own force was on its western flank and another Macabbean group was sited beyond the camp. He thought quickly and changed his plan to divide his troops into three units, one of which advanced against the Seleucid cavalry: the other two made for the phalanx, which they penetrated at its weakest point. The Seleucids hadn't expected to be attacked as they believed their commander, Georgias, was pursuing the Macabbeans in the hills. When the Macabbeans appeared, they panicked and, seeing their phalanx had been demolished, fled.

"The Gentiles (Seleucids) were crushed," recorded the first book of Macabees (Chapter 4, Verses 14-16), "and fled into the plain and all those in the rear fell by the sword. They (the Macabees) pursued them to Gazara and to the plains of Idumea and the Azotus and Jamina, and 3,000 of them fell." The Seleucid camp was plundered and set on fire.

Georgias seems to have realized his pursuit of the small rearguard was fruitless and decided to return to his camp. As soon as they saw their camp in flames, his men panicked in their turn and fled toward the Mediterranean coast.

A third resounding victory for Judas' guerrillas brought large numbers of Jewish fighters to join his army. A year later, in 164BC, Judas' expanded forces engaged the Seleucids for a fourth time, at Beth-Zur, where the former regent and royal viceroy, Lysias, was in command of an army of 20,000 infantry and 4,000 cavalry. Lysias first marched to Askalon along the coast road and then headed for Hebron. The Seleucids built a camp near Hebron and moved north toward Jerusalem.

Judas, however, was already waiting for them. Lysias and his army were caught in an ambush in a defile near Beth Zur, where they were attacked from the surrounding high ground and from below, in the ravines. The Seleucids hastily retreated back to Hebron, where they did not pause for long, for the Judean forces were in hot pursuit. They departed for the coast before the Macabbeans could catch up with them and attack their camp. Not long after this fourth successive victory over his forces, King Antiochus IV Epiphanes died.

After Beth Zur, Judas and his victorious army entered Jerusalem to be greeted by a population almost hysterical with joy. Judas ordered that the Temple, which had been defiled by Greek sacrifices, must be ritually cleansed with oil to restore its holy condition. Subsequently, the Temple was rededicated to God. But Judas was intent on much more than that. He meant to clear the Seleucids out of Jerusalem entirely. He forced what was left of the Seleucid garrison to withdraw to the Acra fortress, the citadel built by Antiochus IV Epiphanes after he captured Jerusalem in 168BC.

This time, though, there was no easy success for Judas and his Macabbeans. The Acra fortress, sited on a hill facing the Temple, was strategically placed to resist assault and the most Judas could do was lay siege to it. Two years later, the siege was still in place, but the Seleucid garrison had implemented a plan to have it raised. They had managed to get a message to Lysias, who set out for Jerusalem on a rescue mission in 162BC with 50,000 infantry and 32 elephants.

Lysias had learned a great deal about how to fight the Macabbeans. Most importantly, he realized how to neutralize the guerrilla tactics that had enabled Judas to trounce his armies four times in succession. Some of the troops he brought with him were there for the sole task of protecting his flanks.

Judas was obliged to abandon his siege and undertake what he had once studiously avoided: a pitched battle against a force that was superior to his own in both armament and numbers. The results of the confrontation at Beth-Zechariah in 162BC were not entirely favorable. Lysias' elephants represented a danger the Macabbeans had never faced before, and although their line held for a

Hasmonean rule

▨ Maccabean territory in 135 BC

▤ Approximate boundary of the
kingdom of Alexander Jannaeus

☙ Greek city taken or destroyed by Jannaeus

◻ Fortress

Sidon

Damascus

Tyre

ITUREA

Antiochia

PHOENICIA

Ptolemais
(Acco)

Seleucia

Great Sea

*Sea of Chinnereth
(Sea of Galilee)*

GALILEE

Western Sea

Plain of Jezreel

Philoteria

Hippos

Yarmuk

Abila

Dium

Dora

Gadara

Strato's Tower

Scythopolis
(Bethshan)

Ephron

Pella

SAMARIA

ARABS

Samaria

Sichem

Amathus

Gerasa

Apollonia

Mt. Gerizim

Zarqa

Joppa

Alexandrium

Jazer

Adida

Modin

Philadelphia
(Rabbatamana)

Port of the Jamnites

Gazara

Michmas

JUDAEA

Jamnia

Jericho

Ashdod

Jerusalem

Hyrcania

Medaba

Ashkelon

Marisa

Bethsura

*Salt Sea
(Dead Sea)*

Macherus

Anthedon

Adora

Hebron

*Arabian
Desert*

Gaza

Masada

IDUMAEA

Raphia

NABATAEANS

N e g e v

NABATAEANS

0   20 km

0   20 miles

*Above: Judas won a series of victories against the
Greek armies, including taking Jerusalem.*

time, Judas was soon on the brink of withdrawing.

But Judas' brother suspected Lysias was on the back of a particularly large elephant: if he could be killed, his forces would lose heart. He manouvered under the elephant and stabbed upward with a spear. The elephant died, but so did Judas' brother when the massive beast fell on top of him. As it turned out, Lysias was not in the howdah, so his sacrifice was in vain. Judas' plan to withdraw went ahead. Gathering his army, he retreated to Jerusalem and returned to Gophna.

Beth-Zechariah was not a defeat, but it was a disappointment and a blow to morale. Judas's army shrank as many of his troops opted to go home. For his last battle, at Elasa, he was left with few more than 3,000 soldiers to confront the next Seleucid general. Bacchides moved against Jerusalem with 20,000 infantry and 4,000 cavalry. The mere sight of the force was enough for 2,000 of Judas' forces to desert, leaving 800 to face the onslaught. They fought so valiantly that they managed to push back Bacchides' right wing, but there was little doubt of the final outcome. The Macabbeans were defeated and Judas was killed.

After the death of Judas, leadership of the Macabbeans passed to his brother, Jonathan, then to another brother, Simon, who became High Priest and a prince of Israel. In 140BC, Simon founded the Hasmonean dynasty, named after a long-ago ancestor, Asmoneus. The dynasty was recognized by the Roman senate and ruled for 103 years until it was taken over by the Roman nominee, Herod the Great.

The Siege of Jerusalem, 70AD

In 66AD, 129 years after the Roman general Gnaeus Pompeius (Pompey) established Judea as a province of the Roman Empire, an accumulation of affronts to the Israelite (Jewish) religion sparked a large-scale rebellion. This uprising culminated, four years later, in a hard-fought siege of Jerusalem, during which over a million of the city's civilians were reportedly killed and the city and its temple were destroyed.

It was, unfortunately, all too easy for pagan conquerors – such as the Romans – to collide with proud, devout monotheists like the Jews of Judea. Although the Romans allowed the Jews to follow their own faith, they never really understood their tenacious devotion to it. Several blunders stemmed from this lack of understanding, but the worst affront came in 39AD, when the more than half-mad Roman emperor Caligula decreed that as a self-proclaimed god, his statue should stand in all temples within his empire. The Jews regarded this as

Opposite: After many years of isolation, the walls of Jerusalem were rebuilt under the supervision of the prophet Nehemiah.

REBUILDING THE WALLS OF JERUSALEM

the ultimate blasphemy, and talk of rebellion was in the air. Although Caligula was assassinated two years later, the rebellious mood simmered for almost 30 years until it finally erupted in 66AD. Greeks were seen sacrificing birds in front of the synagogue and the High Priest in Jerusalem retaliated by refusing to offer prayers and make sacrifices in honor of the Roman emperor Nero. Soon afterward, the Jews mounted an attack on a Roman garrison in Jerusalem and killed a large number of legionairies. The fires of rebellion were well and truly lit.

From then on, the uprising spread throughout Judea, and, at first, the rebels scored some successes. They destroyed the Romans' debt archives, and when Gaius Cestius Gallus, the Roman commander in neighboring Syria, marched his XII Legion to Jerusalem, he met with such ferocious resistance that he was obliged to retreat. The Jews pursued him and at the pass of Bethhoron, some 6,000 of Gallus' soldiers were killed and the eagle of the XII Legion was captured.

Despite this triumph, which greatly boosted Jewish morale, the reality was that the Roman army was the greatest and most successful military force in the ancient world. Besides this, Emperor Nero knew he could not afford to let the Judean rebels set a bad example that might be followed by other provinces of his empire. Nero therefore appointed Titus Flavius Vespasianus, an experienced commander and provincial governor, to put down the unrest.

But before Vespasianus could embark on his task, Nero lost the support of the senate in Rome and even of his own Praetorian Guard. In 68AD, he committed suicide. Vespasianus became caught up in the subsequent civil war, which involved four candidates for the imperial crown. Vespasianus, who was one of them, eventually prevailed and returned to Judea in 70AD as Emperor Vespasian. He brought with him his 27-year-old son Titus Flavius, himself a future emperor, as the Roman field commander and, despite his comparative youth, a seasoned fighter and skilled leader of men.

With the arrival of Vespasian and Titus, the Zealots, the Jewish revolutionaries, were obliged to set aside their own internecine squabbles and co-operate to face the danger.

Titus Flavius commanded 40,000 troops comprising four legions, together with detachments from Egypt and Syria and local auxiliaries. The two Zealot groups and another group led by Simon bar Giora fielded 24,000 well-equipped, fiercely motivated men.

The task that confronted the Romans was formidable. Jerusalem was heavily fortified, with the Temple of Solomon surrounded by strong walls and two hills as natural strongpoints close to the city.

From the start, Titus intended to besiege Jerusalem before mounting an assault, and he made his preparations in the standard Roman fashion. First order of business was the construction of a secure camp, but the work was twice interrupted by Zealots, who mounted surprise attacks on the legionaries from the eastern side of the city. It took a mighty effort to beat them off and assume control but, eventually,

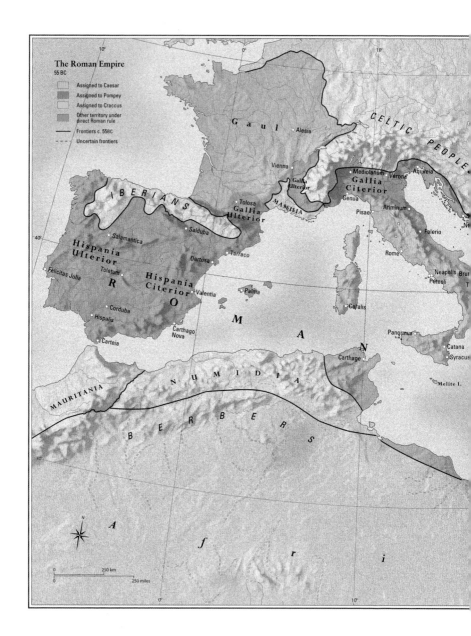

The Roman Empire
55 BC

Assigned to Caesar
Assigned to Pompey
Assigned to Craccus
Other territory under
direct Roman rule
——— Frontiers c. 55BC
- - - Uncertain frontiers

G a u l

Alesia

CELTIC PEOPLE

Vienna

Mediolanum
Verona
Aquileia

Gallia
Citerior

Gallia
Ulterior

Genua

Ariminum

Pisae

IBERIANS

Tolosa

Gallia
Ulterior

MASSILIA

Salduba

Falerio

Salamantica

Rome

Tarraco

Hispania
Ulterior
R

Toletum

Dertosa

Neapolis Brur

Felicitas Julia

Peteoli

Hispania
Citerior
O

Valentia

Palma

Corduba

Caralis

Hispalis

M

Carthago
Nova

A

Panormus

Carteia

Catana
Syracus

Carthage

N

Melite I.

MAURITANIA

N U M I D I A

B E R B E R S

A

f

r

i

192 Battles of the Bible

Left: During the time of the New Testament, the Roman Empire was already reaching its impressive peak, with visible traces of Roman rule throughout Europe and beyond.

the Romans managed to establish their siege.

The rebels, however, had no intention of letting the Romans enjoy an easy time while they waited for the normal depredations of a siege – starvation, disease, despair – to work in their favor. Time and again, they ventured out, on one occasion luring some of the soldiers with false offers of surrender, then attacking them with a storm of missiles. Spurred to action, Titus Flavius decided to break into Jerusalem through its third defensive wall. This involved, first of all, setting up a barrage of covering fire from missiles while the soldiers cleared the ground and amassed a supply of timber. While this went on, the rebels plastered them with missiles from scorpions and ballistas, which they had captured from the garrison in Jerusalem. The Romans fired back with their own siege machines.

The exchange of fire continued until Titus Flavius realized it would not be possible to breach the walls of Jerusalem with missiles alone. Instead, the Romans brought in battering rams and constructed three ramps to "climb" the walls so that they could batter away through the stonework from the top. As longstanding Roman experience of sieges had revealed, it was usually a sraightforward matter to batter a way through the walls once the ramps had been completed. And so it proved. The rebel forces tried everything to throw back the Roman assault – shooting the crews manning the rams or burning the rams themselves – but, eventually,

Opposite: If defended with zeal, Jerusalem was fortified heavily enough to withstand long sieges by the greatest of military powers.

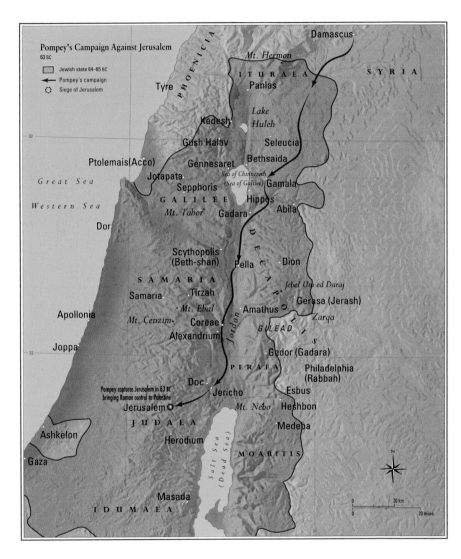

Above: Pompey captured Jerusalem in 63BC,
ending just 100 years of Jewish independence.

after 15 days, the wall was breached and the Romans stormed through.

The Zealots realized at once that the third wall was lost and, although some resolved to go on fighting, the rest retreated to the second wall to mount further resistance. But history merely repeated itself, as the Romans once more erected their battering rams and, despite fanatical efforts from the Zealots, managed to breach the second wall in turn. This time, they did it in only five days. Titus personally led a crack force of 1,000 men through the breach, but they were once again ferociously attacked – so much so that they had to fight their way out through the streets and withdraw.

The Zealots were able to enjoy their triumph for only three days before the Romans returned and, this time, barged their way through the breach and forced the defenders to fall back. Titus Flavius ordered that the breach be made wider and guards be placed around it to deter further attacks.

As an experienced commander, Titus realized the next fortification his forces must tackle – the first wall around Jerusalem – would be the hardest and most costly to overcome. This was the Great Temple, a holy place of immense significance for Jews, and the tower, known as the Fortress of Antonia, that stood at one corner. It was a truly mighty fortification, with walls over 30 meters thick and a height of some 22 meters. The Romans again built their ramps, this time against the walls of the fortress, but the Zealots had learned a trick or two from their experiences. Although the Romans completed the ramps

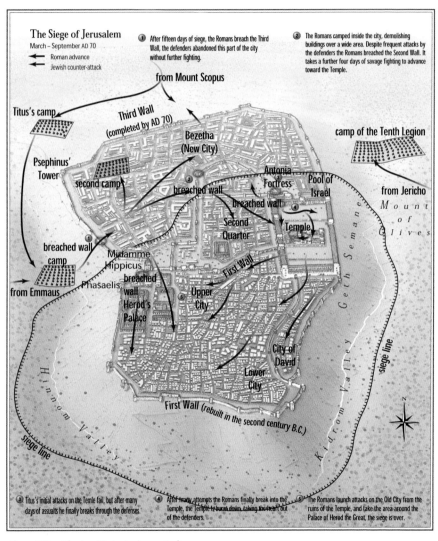

The Siege of Jerusalem

March – September AD 70

← Roman advance
← Jewish counter-attack

① After fifteen days of siege, the Romans breach the Third Wall, the defenders abandoned this part of the city without further fighting.

② The Romans camped inside the city, demolishing buildings over a wide area. Despite frequent attacks by the defenders the Romans breached the Second Wall. It takes a further four days of savage fighting to advance toward the Temple.

from Mount Scopus

Titus's camp

Third Wall (completed by AD 70)

Bezetha (New City)

camp of the Tenth Legion

Psephinus' Tower

second camp

breached wall

Antonia Fortress

Pool of Israel

from Jericho

Mount of Olives

breached wall

Second Quarter

Temple

breached wall camp

Mirıamme Hippicus

breached wall

Phasaelis

Herod's Palace

First Wall

Upper City

City of David

Lower City

Hinnom Valley

Geth Semane

Kidron Valley

siege line

N

from Emmaus

First Wall (rebuilt in the second century B.C.)

siege line

③ Titus's initial attacks on the Temle fail, but after many days of assaults he finally breaks through the defenses.

④ After many attempts the Romans finally break into the Temple, the Temple is burnt down, taking the heart out of the defenders.

⑤ The Romans launch attacks on the Old City from the ruins of the Temple, and take the area around the Palace of Herod the Great, the siege is over.

Above: Titus Flavius, Vespasion's son, took over the siege of Jerusalem when his father became emperor.

in 17 days, they found them collapsing into the earth as they fell into mine tunnels secretly dug by the Zealots without any of them noticing. The rebels backed this up with an attack on the Roman camp, which both dismayed and demoralized Titus Flavius' forces.

Titus knew he couldn't afford to fail, for his father's prestige as well as his own was at stake. He devised a new approach. He ordered his troops to build their own fortification to surround the entire city. The work was completed in only three days. Now, the Zealots were doubly besieged. They were unable to slip out of the city to forage for food – and by now, food was growing short. In addition, if they could not get out past the ring of Roman fortifications, no aid could get in.

The Romans resumed building their siege ramps against the walls of the Fortress of Antonia. Within three weeks they were finished and, despite Zealot forays to destroy them, the rams were able to start operating.

Already weakened by the mine tunnels dug by the rebels, the Tower collapsed, leaving a wide breach, but one that the Romans found was backed by a makeshift wall. The resistance here was so stiff that it took the Romans three determined assaults, involving hand-to-hand fighting in the courtyard of the Temple, before they prevailed and the position was secured.

Now, the Temple, the holiest structure in all Jerusalem, lay before the Romans and, because of its significance, it was defended with a fervor that transcended anything that had gone before. The Zealots launched raid after fanatical raid against them, but the

Roman infantry, supported by cavalry, gradually battered their way through the temple in a series of close-quarter fights until they reached the Inner Court. By this time, the Temple had caught fire after a Roman legionary threw a flaming torch at the walls. The fire spread through the Temple complex and beyond into the residential areas around it and continued to burn as the rebels were forced out and the Romans finally took charge.

The Zealots were now down to their last redoubt, the Old City of Jerusalem, which lay beyond what was now the smoking wreckage of the Temple. Once more, the Romans built their ramps. But by this time, the defenders of Jerusalem were hungry, sick, and demoralized. They were barely able to make yet another stand against Titus' men, and most of them scattered and fled before the Romans could come to grips with them.

On September 7, 70AD, the siege of Jerusalem came to an end. Several rebel leaders including Simon bar Giora and the Zealot John of Gischala, were captured but others managed to get away from Jerusalem through underground tunnels.

Although the Romans hunted for these rebel leaders, many managed to elude their pursuers and headed for other areas around the Mediterranean. Zealots who remained free, though fugitive, in Judea lost none of their resolve to resist Rome at all costs. Those who lived to fight another day made another, last stand three years after the fall of Jerusalem, at the fortress of Masada, in what is now southern Israel.

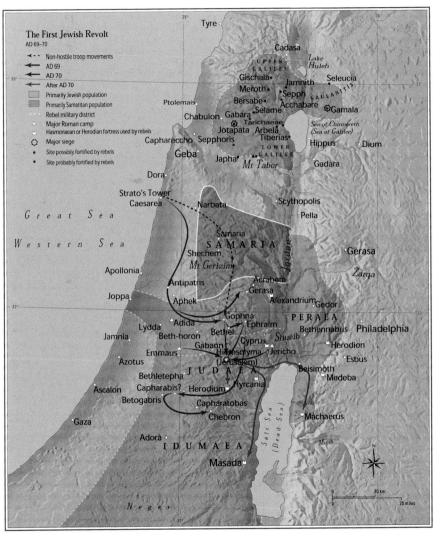

The First Jewish Revolt
AD 69–70

◀- - Non-hostile troop movements
◀── AD 69
◀── AD 70
◀── After AD 70
▢ Primarily Jewish population
▢ Primarily Samaritan population
- - - Rebel military district
△ Major Roman camp
⬢ Hasmonaean or Herodian fortress used by rebels
◯ Major siege
• Site possibly fortified by rebels
• Site probably fortified by rebels

Tyre
Cadasa
UPPER GALILEE
Lake Huleh
Gischala
Jamnith
Seleucia
Meroth
Sepph
GAULANITIS
Bersabe
Acchabare
Gamala
Ptolemais
Chabulon
Gabara
Selame
Tarichaeae
Sea of Chinnereth (Sea of Galilee)
Jotapata
Arbela
Caphareccho
Sepphoris
Tiberias
LOWER GALILEE
Hippus
Dium
Geba
Japha
Mt Tabor
Gadara
Dora
Strato's Tower
Caesarea
Narbata
Scythopolis
Great Sea
Pella
Western Sea
Samaria
Gerasa
SAMARIA
Shechem
Mt Gerizim
Zarqa
Apollonia
Acrabeta
Antipatris
Gerasa
Joppa
Aphek
Alexandrium
Gedor
Gophna
PERAEA
Lydda
Adida
Ephraim
Bethennabris
Philadelphia
Jamnia
Beth-horon
Bethel
Cyprus
Shueib
Herodion
Emmaus
Gabaon
Hierosolyma
Jericho
Esbus
Azotus
(Jerusalem)
Bethletepha
JUDAEA
Beisimoth
Capharabis?
Herodium
Hyrcania
Medeba
Ascalon
Bethogabris
Capharatobas
Salt Sea (Dead Sea)
Machaerus
Gaza
Chebron
Adora
IDUMAEA
Mujib
Masada
Negev

0   20 km
0   20 miles

*Above: Jewish resistance to the Romans began
in Caesarea and ended with Masada's bitter,
bloody fall.*

King Herod the Great

Herod was one of the most detested monarchs of all time. He was hated for his cruelty, murders, and the "slaughter of the innocents". He was hated, too, for the removal of his Hasmonean predecessor and his status as a "creature" of the Roman conquerors. Nevertheless, he remained king for 33 years, attempting to commend himself with magnificent building projects, boosting the economy, and expanding religious sites.

Herod was the first non-Jewish king of Judea – another of the many reasons why he was disliked – and how he came by his kingdom, with Roman backing, was not likely to win the hearts of his subjects. Judea had already become a province of the vast Roman Empire a quarter of a century before Herod went to Rome to obtain it for himself. In Rome, Herod presented himself before the Senate and Octavius Caesar – soon to become Augustus, the first Roman emperor – and persuaded them to back his candidature. He returned to the Jewish kingdom accompanied

Above: Herod was despised for many reasons, the most famous of which was his slaughter of the innocents of Bethlehem, described in the Book of Matthew (Chapter 2, Verses 16-18). As the 19th-century German historian Heinrich Gräz said of Herod, he was the "evil genius" of Judea – despite the good works he tried to do, opinion of him remains opprobrius many centuries later.

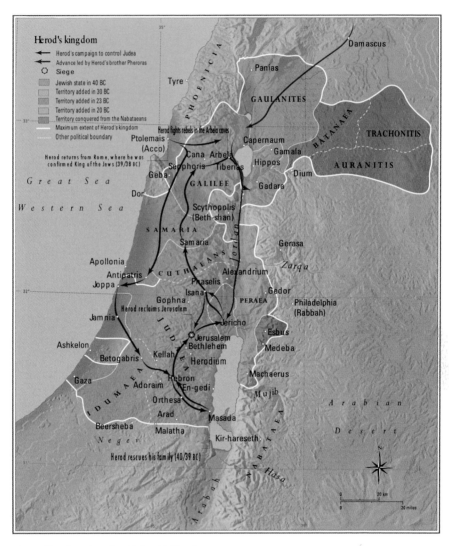

Herod's kingdom

→ Herod's campaign to control Judea
→ Advance led by Herod's brother Pheroras
○ Siege

Jewish state in 40 BC
Territory added in 30 BC
Territory added in 23 BC
Territory added in 20 BC
Territory conquered from the Nabataeans
Maximum extent of Herod's kingdom
Other political boundary

Herod returns from Rome, where he was confirmed King of the Jews (39/38 BC)

Herod fights rebels in the Arbela caves

Herod reclaims Jerusalem

Herod rescues his family (40/39 BC)

Damascus

PHOENICIA

Panias

Tyre

GAULANITES

BATANAEA

TRACHONITIS

Ptolemais
(Acco)

Capernaum

Gamala

AURANITIS

Cana Arbela

Sepphoris   Tiberias

Hippos

Dium

Geba

GALILEE

Gadara

Dor

Scythopolis
(Beth-shan)

Great Sea

Western Sea

SAMARIA

Samaria

Gerasa

Jordan

Zarqa

Apollonia

Antipatris

CUTHAEANS

Alexandrium

Joppa

Phaselis

Gedor

Isana

PERAEA

Philadelphia
(Rabbah)

Gophna

Jamnia

Jericho

Ashkelon

Kellah

Jerusalem
Bethlehem

Esbus

Medeba

Betogabris

Herodium

Machaerus

Gaza

Adoraim

Hebron
En-gedi

Mujib

Arabian

Orthesa

Arad

Masada

Desert

NABATAEA

Beersheba

Malatha

Kir-hareseth

Hasa

Negev

IDUMAEA

JUDAEA

Arabah

0   20 km
0   20 miles

N

*Above: Herod consistently added to his kingdom
during his reign, between the years of 40BC
and 20BC.*

by two Roman legions; they proceeded to lay siege to Jerusalem to remove the incumbent, Antigonus, the last king of the Hasmonean dynasty. The Romans conducted the siege with their customary efficiency and ruthlessness and the defeated Antigonus was taken in chains to Rome, where he was executed.

The Hasmoneans, the descendants of the valiant Macabbees, were greatly revered by the Jews so that, in their eyes, Herod was from the first a villain and usurper. Unfortunately, Herod bolstered this image with atrocity. His assumption of the throne was resisted by Jews, who refused to acknowledge him as king. They took shelter in mountain caves, where they were later besieged by Herod's troops. Some were tempted out of hiding by Herod's offer of a pardon, but those who refused suffered horrific fates. According to the Jewish historian Josephus, some were shot with darts, others hauled out of the caves by means of hooks and thrown over the mountain precipice. Others were simply killed where they had attempted to hide. To force out the last survivors, the caves were set on fire. One old man killed his seven children rather than let them surrender to Herod and afterward threw himself into the ravine below.

This cruelty inevitably spawned numerous plots to kill Herod. None succeeded, but nevertheless Herod became obsessed with security. In fact, he built Masada, the giant fortress in the Judean desert, as a bolt-hole for himself in case his subjects rebelled against him. Not content with Masada itself, Herod constructed a ring of other fortresses as further insurance. He built castles as well as palaces in Jerusalem, Jericho, Sepphoris in Galilee and other fortified bases in Perea and Ascalon, all to ensure his army would be able to defend both Masada and their king against all comers.

Herod's army, which at its peak comprised 40,000 men, was an impressive force, equipped with the latest weaponry and both highly trained and disciplined. Apart from providing Herod with quality garrisons for his forts and fortresses, the army proved irresistible against the Nabatean Arabs, who were destroyed in a war fought in 32-31BC. Herod's navy was no less imposing and, as he intended, helped to give his kingdom an image of military might.

A great deal of the care Herod lavished on his kingdom was done to woo his subjects and cool the persistent enmity with which they regarded him. He founded entire cities, constructed sports centers, theatres, aqueducts, ports, and roads. In 25BC, he organized massive imports of grain to stave off a threatened famine. At the same time, Herod reduced taxes by one-third, which should have been a popular move. In 20BC, he began the expansion of the Temple of Jerusalem to quell complaints that his own palace, nearby, dominated the hallowed place of worship. The rebuilding program lasted for ten years and involved 10,000 workmen. To protect the sensibilities of the Jews, 1,000 priests were hired to ensure that only they could enter the sacred areas of the Temple.

By 14BC, after 23 years on the throne, Herod was able to expand his activities – and

Herod's Building Projects

- ◆ Site of Herod's building projects or military installation
- ⚓ Port
- ▨ Extent of Herod's kingdom

36°

ITUREA

PHOENICIA

SYRIA

◆ Caesarea-Philippi (Panias)

GAULANITES

Lake Huleh

BATANAEA

TRACHONITIS

Sea of Chinnereth (Sea of Galilee)

AURANITIS

33°

G r e a t   S e a

◆ Sepphoris
◆ Geba   GALILEE
Mt Tabor

W e s t e r n   S e a

◆ Agrippina

Caesarea
(Strato's Tower) ⚓◆

SAMARIA

Samaria was rebuilt as Sebaste to honour Augustus   ◆ Sebaste (Samaria)
◆ Amathus

Mt Gerizim

Qiryat Bene Hassan ◆   C U T H A E A N S   ◆ Alexandrium

Antipatris ◆   Phaselis ◆

32°

Herod's main palace and new temple were located in Jerusalem

Doc (Docus)   Herod's royal palace
Threx ◆
◆ Cypros   ◆ Jericho ◆ Livias (Beth-ramatha)
Jerusalem ◆   ◆ Esbus

Ashkelon ◆   J U D A E A   ◆ Hyrcania

◆ Herodium

Agrippium ⚓   I D U M A E A   ◆ Hebron   ◆ Machaerus

A r a b i a n

◆ Masada
Herod's rock fortress

D e s e r t

Malatha ◆

N e g e v

Salt Sea (Dead Sea)

Arabah   *Aqaba*

20 km
20 miles

*Above: Herod was a great builder, of both military
installations and other magnificent structures, in
the name of both safety and glorification.*

King Herod the Great   207

his attempts to win over his subjects – by aiding Jews living outside Judea. The Jews living in nearby Anatolia and Cyrene were being hard-pressed by their rulers, but Herod's treasury was now large and rich enough for him to give them substantial aid. He also used his influence to persuade the Romans to protect Jewish rights within their colonies. For a second time, in 14BC, Herod reduced taxes in Judea.

One of the Jewish sects, the

Below: Herod built a palace for himself on the Wadi Qilt, just south of the site on which Jericho had once stood.

Sadducees, seemed convinced by Herod's shows of generosity and goodwill, but their rivals, the Pharisees, remained aloof. This was hardly surprising since King Herod was dissipating his own efforts by a series of atrocities that no amount of good works could disguise.

In 6BC, Herod executed several Pharisee leaders when they predicted the event that would bring his reign to an end: the birth in Bethlehem of the Messiah, the savior who, by tradition, all Jews awaited for a glorious era on Earth to be inaugurated. This, it seems, confirmed the prediction that Herod was supposed to have received from the Magi, the three wise men.

However, the slaughter of all the male infants in Bethlehem, to make sure the Messiah would be slaughtered among them, was only one of Herod's many attrocities. In 4BC, young students of the Torah, the first five books of the Hebrew scriptures, tore down the golden Roman eagle sited over the main entrance to the Temple; for this, Herod had 40 of them, together with two of their teachers, burned alive.

Even Herod's own family was not safe from him. He had two of his sons executed for plotting against him, and also executed Mariamne, one of his ten wives, on a trumped-up charge of adultery, together with her mother Alexandra and her brother Kostobar.

Doubtless to the relief of the majority of the Judean people, Herod died in 4BC; one of the derogatory sentiments voiced on hearing the news came from the Roman Emperor Augustus himself, who remarked: "It would be better to be Herod's pig than his son".

The Fall of Masada, 72AD

After the Jewish rebellion was crushed by the Romans, small pockets of resistance remained in Judea. Most were put down by the Roman army and control was restored, but the mote in the eye of Roman success was the most determined resistance of all, at Masada, in the Judean desert, near the Dead Sea. The Zealots and other rebels who holed themselves up in this mighty fortress were resolved to die to the last man, woman, and child rather than submit to Roman rule.

The word 'Masada' means fortress in Hebrew; the mighty stronghold stood at the top of a rocky outcrop some 50 meters above sea level. But since it was sited by the Dead Sea, the world's lowest land area, it was much further out of reach, at 449 meters above the surrounding countryside. The cliffs on its eastern side stood 396 meters high; the casement wall around the top of the 150,000-square meter plateau was 1,500 meters long and four meters thick. Three pathways led up to the plateau, but any attempt to climb them was virtual suicide, for Masada's

Above: Masada was a virtually impregnable fortress, looming 449m above the landscape. It had few entrances, which made it easy to guard.

defenders were always in a position to pour down a deadly barrage of missiles from above.

Masada boasted several towers, storehouses, barracks, an armory, and a palace to cater for the lavish lifestyle of Herod, who constructed the fortress almost a century before the Zealots arrived there. For Herod, a much-hated monarch, Masada was a bolt-hole where he could shelter if his subjects rebelled against him. It was, therefore, pure irony that his fortress became the last bastion of the Jewish rebellion.

It seems that the extremist Sicarii, under the command of

Above: Reservoirs were cut into the rock to keep Masada supplied with water, adding to the mighty fortress's self-sustainability.

Jews in Jerusalem and been thrown out of the city as a consequence. Three or four years later, when the Zealot survivors of the siege of Jerusalem were forced out in turn, they naturally headed for Masada. By the time the Romans arrived to retrieve the fortress, in 72AD, it housed around 1,000 fighting men, vastly augmented by their wives and families. From time to time, the rebels ventured beyond its massive walls to harass and raid the Roman settlements in the surrounding countryside. In one settlement, Ein Gedi, which was inhabited by Jews, the Sicarii are said to have killed 700 people. But, inevitably, these forays came to an end once the Emperor

Elazar ben Ya'ir, seized Masada near the start of the rebellion, after mounting a surprise attack on the garrison. They were afterwards joined by more Sicarii, who had quarreled with more moderate-minded

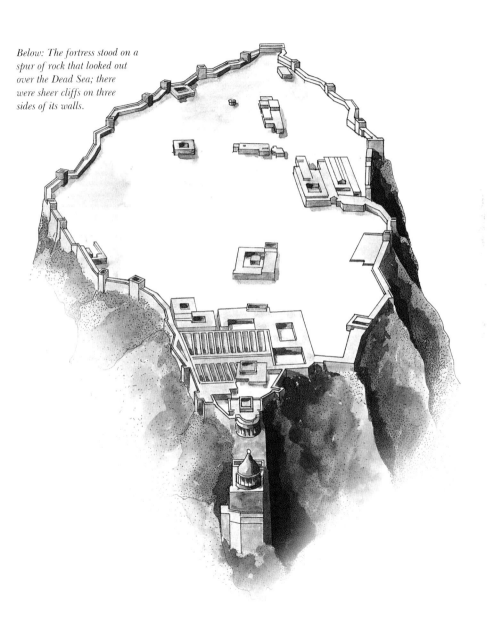

Below: The fortress stood on a spur of rock that looked out over the Dead Sea; there were sheer cliffs on three sides of its walls.

Vespasian demanded the reduction of Masada and the destruction of its defenders.

The Roman X Legion, commanded by Lucius Flavius Silva, governor of Judea, numbered 7,000 experienced soldiers who had fought at the siege of Jerusalem. They were particularly noted for their expertise with siege engines, a skill that was going to be especially valuable at Masada. Flavius Silva soon discovered that the Zealots and Sicarii were in no mood to surrender: in fact, they flatly refused. In addition, the tactics of stealth, deception, and surprise might be effective in other, easier, contexts but were out of the question when the challenge was such a formidable fortress.

It was also true, however, that the Romans had distinct advantages. The rest of Judea had been pacified, so there was no chance the defenders could be relieved by other rebels. There was no one to attack the Romans or disrupt their supply lines and the Zealots and Sicarii had no chance of escape should it occur to them to run away. The Romans could take their time, and prepared their assault with the supreme confidence of a force that, historically, may have lost the occasional battle, but never a war.

Their first task was to build a secure camp and encircle it with a heavily fortified wall. Next, the Romans organized an army of slaves to bring in a stream of supplies, which they knew could not be interrupted either by the defenders, who were sealed inside Masada, or by guerrillas in the surrounding desert.

Turning to the business of mounting a viable assault, the X Legion made the only logical choice: an enormous siege ramp capable of "climbing" the soaring walls and so affording the Romans entry into the fortress. The materials the Romans required were all around them in the Judean desert, with its plentiful supply of rocks, which they crushed and covered with earth. The ramp, probably the largest and loftiest ramp they had ever constructed, was 100 metres high. The Romans started building in the autumn of 73AD and took around six months to complete the task, in the spring of 74AD.

Now, the Romans were able to push a siege tower up the ramp, until it was against the fortress wall. The tower, which was 30 metres tall, contained a ram together with positions for troops whose task it was to protect it. As the ram got going, battering away at the wall, the Romans used their other siege engines to give it heavy covering fire. The engines also served to ensure the defenders were kept away from the ram and could do nothing to prevent it breaching the wall.

It was, however, a slow business that gave the defenders time to construct a defense line, using heavy wooden beams covered in earth. Eventually, the Romans cracked the wall and entered Masada through the breach, only to come up against the makeshift defense line, which was lined with men determined to fight to the death there and then. Their defense was so savage and the Romans had so much trouble removing them that, in the end, Flavius Silva ordered his men to set it on fire. The fire took some time to burn through, and while it was doing so, the Roman siege machines were only a meter or two away from being set ablaze.

But then, the wind changed direction and fanned the flames so that the beams burned more quickly. The heat was intense and the Romans stood back until, at last, the beams collapsed into ashes. This was the point at which the Zealots and Sicarii were finally forced to concede that they had lost Masada. With the Romans about to storm through, the defenders and their families faced the fearful fate of being put to the sword. The alternatives were hardly less grim: crucifixion, the standard Roman punishment for rebels and traitors, or being sold into slavery.

No one inside Masada wanted to hand the Romans a triumph of this humiliating nature, so they resorted to the only possible way out: a suicide pact. Normally, suicide was – and still is – forbidden to Jews on the grounds that it was the ultimate wickedness and an offense against God, the Creator and giver of life. So arrangements were made for there to be only one suicide, by the last man left alive. The defenders drew lots to select ten candidates who would kill all the other men, women, and children. That done, one of the ten would kill the other nine and then kill himself.

But before the deaths took place, Elazar ben Ya'ir ordered everything destroyed except the food stores, to show that the defenders had not chosen death because of starvation but had embraced it as the only honorable way out of their dilemma. In addition, Masada was to be set on fire, so that the Romans would in no way benefit from its capture. Not all of the fortress was consumed, but the point was made. Then, the killings began.

When the Romans finally penetrated Masada, they heard no sound or movement, only a pall of deathly silence. Picking their way through the streets and buildings, the Romans found bodies everywhere – young, old, male, female, all of them were dead. Even the legionairies, accustomed to death and the ravages of war, were shocked at the sight. The only survivors were two women and five

*Above: The Romans surrounded the fortress of
Masada with walls and forts of their own.*

children, who hid themselves in a water cistern as the mass killing went on outside. It was through them that the story of Masada and what happened there became known.

With the fall of Masada, the "Great Rebellion" of 66-74AD came to its close. But it was not the last Jewish revolt against Roman rule. Another uprising occurred some 60 years later, between 132AD and 135AD, and though it was, inevitably, crushed, the Romans found Judea so difficult to control that the X Legion, already assigned to police the province, had to be augmented by a second legion. Masada, meanwhile, became and remains a symbol of Jewish defiance to all invaders and occupiers and the subject of an oath sworn by Israeli soldiers today: "Masada," it warns, "shall never fall again".

Index